ALL IN
TOGETHER
RHYMES, DITTIES, AND JINGLES
OF NEWFOUNDLAND AND LABRADOR

ROBIN MCGRATH

BOULDER
PUBLICATIONS

All In Together: Rhymes, Ditties, and Jingles of Newfoundland and Labrador / Robin McGrath.

ISBN 978-0-9783381-9-0

1. Folk poetry, Canadian (English) – Newfoundland and Labrador. 2. Canadian poetry (English) – Newfoundland and Labrador. I. McGrath, Robin

PS8379.N49A44 2009   398.809718   C2009-902295-8

Published by Boulder Publications
Portugal Cove-St. Philip's, Newfoundland and Labrador

www.boulderpublications.ca

Design and layout by John Andrews and Granite Studios

Printed in Canada

We acknowledge the financial support of the Government of Newfoundland and Labrador through the Department of Tourism, Culture and Recreation.

Newfoundland
Labrador

For the grandchildren, Robbie, Alex, Emily Leah, Elizabeth, and Erin; John Michael, Jacqueline, Seumas, Kathleen, Oscar, and Sydney Jane; Theo and Christian; Erin Brett, Liam, Jonah, Cheyenne, Rafi, Katelin, Jake, Joseph, Eloise, and Jorja Rae; Maggie, Sían, Lewis, Fuzzy, and Ella; Olivia, Dylan, Eleanor, Owen and Finlay; Rebecca, Melissa, Misha, and Aiden; Jacob; and those yet to arrive.

All in together,
All kinds of weather!

Introduction

As one of the youngest of a large family, I grew up with nursery rhymes coming at me from all sides. My parents, sisters and brothers, aunts and uncles, and the principal teacher at the little school I attended all believed in decorating even the most common exchanges with ditties, fragments of verse, limericks, parodies, riddles, counting games, and catch phrases. A surprising number of these lodged deep in my psyche, and emerged again later in my life.

I am not sure at what point I began to write the verses down. My very earliest notes, made when I was teaching children's literature at the University of Western Ontario in the 1980s, have long been lost, although some of the verses I dredged up from my memory can still be found as marginalia in my classroom copy of Iona and Peter Opie's classic *Oxford Dictionary of Nursery Rhymes*. Others turn up in some of my books, integrated into the texts of both poems and fiction. It wasn't until 2001 that I began to make a determined effort to gather together, between the covers of a single notebook, all the specifically Newfoundland and Labrador verses I recalled or encountered.

In 2004, I published *Nursery Rhymes of Newfoundland and Labrador*, a selection of 300 of the rhymes I had collected. I did not include all the verses I had because some were too repetitive or rhythmically clumsy, and others were frankly rude, racist, or downright dirty. Committing sexist, sexual, and racist remarks to print often makes them more offensive than mere repetition does. The reader's relationship to the page is intensely intimate but, at the same time, it is very public and I found I was uncomfortable with some material when it was denied the context of personal communication.

Contrary to popular belief, nursery rhymes are not written by or for children. They are generally part of the adult world and are co-opted by children who appreciate their simplicity or are merely fascinated by the enigmatic sound of the words. Often the children who repeat these verses don't even know what they mean, and it is probably best left that way. My aim was not to provide a complete compendium but to recreate some of the pleasure and music of my own childhood games, which at a distance of fifty years were lively, instructive, and compelling.

Nursery Rhymes was not an academic volume. I did not want the book to be weighed down by paraphernalia. Even assigning ownership by crediting any one person for his or her contribution seemed wrong. Except where I knew for certain who the author was, I avoided attaching names or sources, because I believed the verses were the property of the people of Newfoundland and Labrador.

Many of these verses came from my own memory, which was often stimulated by finding the same or similar verses in memoirs or community histories. Some of the entries were recited to me at readings, over kitchen tables, on the telephone, or included in letters. I was not alone in my interest in nursery rhymes: Dr. Les Harris's *Growing Up with Verse* put these rhymes into the context of an outport childhood, and Mary Fearon and Lori Fritz's *Over the Big Fat Waves* documented how the rhymes were used in games that involve clapping, chasing, singing, counting, and skipping.

My primary criteria for collecting any particular verse was that it have some identifiable place name, family name, word, phrase, or linguistic structure that identified it as coming from Newfoundland or Labrador. Sometimes I later found the same verse in a collection of English or American verses, but my version generally had some distinctive characteristic that made it our own. In about a dozen cases I included verses that were solely English or Irish in origin, but so widely known in Newfoundland

and Labrador that to omit them would have left a gaping hole in the collection. Some of the verses, found in a number of books, were recited to me with enthusiasm by people of all ages from around the island and across the Straits.

When I published *Nursery Rhymes of Newfoundland and Labrador*, I believed readers would discover, as I did, that the metres, cadences, and general constructions of the rhymes triggered memories, and, in very short order, the chants and games of childhood would come flooding back. How well I succeeded became evident one day shortly after the book came out, when I found myself at the Christmas Craft Fair at the Glacier in Mount Pearl, singing and acting out "King William Was King George's Son" in the middle of the aisle with a group of older women, none of whom I knew but all of whom had the same vivid, visceral memory of the game that I did.

I sold about eighty copies of the book that afternoon, collected another handful of verses, and realized that I might have finished with nursery rhymes but they hadn't finished with me. Four years later, there were double the number of verses I had in the original book and the primary print run was almost sold out. Oddly enough, a number of these unpublished rhymes were from my own memory, verses that had initially resisted the probing process of remembering that I had initiated the first time around. The question of whether to reprint or expand the original edition came up, and I found that the verses had become so entangled with my own recollections of childhood that I was no longer interested in just reproducing the raw material. I felt it needed a context.

Every time contributors gave me a verse, which I scribbled down on a scrap of paper, a napkin, or an old receipt, they also gave me a snapshot of their lives. For instance, Otto Tucker, describing Hemp Seed Night on Midsummer's Eve, told me how he and the other boys of Winterton chased girls on 'The Banks' behind Tucker's

Gardens. The Banks area was also known to be haunted, so there was an overlay of spookiness to the evening. How he laughed when he told me that one little girl allowed herself to be caught by him, because, as she explained, "I trustes you because you're saved."

When I sent a promotional bookmark for *Nursery Rhymes* to my old pen-pal, Gordon Williams, printed with the verse "Love is Like a Head of Cabbage," he was suddenly carried back to December 1, 1931, when his chum Eric Snow had written that verse into his friendship book. Gordon and Eric had been friends at Bishop Feild school and later at Memorial. During the Second World War, Eric joined the Royal Air Force and was lost when his plane was shot down over the Indian Ocean. Just seeing that little verse brought back all Gordon's youthful fondness and grief for Eric, and I had trouble keeping a lump out of my throat when he told me about him.

One of the curious results of collecting these verses was that I not only acquired these second-hand memories, but I also gathered new ones of my own. I collected two verses from Wayne Ledwell while he was renovating a kitchen in Portugal Cove one sunny afternoon. The *Beaumont Hamel* was hooting away in the background, and Wayne's Southern Shore accent grew so thick as he told his story that I had to get him to scribble the words down with a carpenter's pencil on a wooden shingle. I had that shingle propped up over my desk for weeks before I could bring myself to feed it to the fire.

Some of my memories are a complex interweaving of the oral and the literary. I recorded a riddle about a clergyman at Bernice and George Morgan's old family house in Coley's Point, but in my mind the verse is inextricably linked to the day I spent there with their daughter Jennifer, eating chili and talking books with a visiting group of letterset printers. Jennifer's lovely memoir, "A Privilege of Birth," describes a visit to that house with her dying father, and the essay, the chili, and the riddle are all confused in my memory so that I cannot see the verse without missing my own father.

I was not able to complete all the rhymes I chased after. For instance, there was said to be a verse attached to the corpse of Peter Downey, when it was dumped on the doorstep of Dr. Sterling of Harbour Grace in 1834, which began "Doctor, doctor, can you cure / Downey from Gibbet Hill?" Neither could I complete one of the surprisingly few rhymes about J.R. Smallwood, which ended "Now he's in the money and he's doing fine, / With a million dollar ranch on the Roaches Line." By far the most elusive of these incomplete rhymes is one that children learned at school, before Queen Victoria made the pitcher plant our national flower: "Capillaire / Maidenhair … its berry modest and white as snow, / Endurance, purity for show." It was recited to me in full once, but by the time I found a pencil to write it down, it had disappeared forever from the memory of my informant.

If I had it to do again, I would write down not just the verses but also every story that was told to me by the people who gave me verses, and I would put each verse into the context of their lives. Instead, all I have is a scrawled list of names and communities, books and articles, and my own memories of how these and similar verses fitted into my own life. So that is what I offer here. In response to readers' comments and questions, I have also tried to give more information about the rhymes, including explanatory notes about what they might mean and where they came from.

In keeping with my initial determination not to assign ownership to the rhymes, my notes are often incomplete, and, despite my change of heart, I have been unable to backtrack and document my first encounters with many of the rhymes. While I still believe that nobody owns oral literature, I wish for the sake of completeness that I could direct my readers to the specific books, papers, and people that were the sources of my collection. The bibliography is incomplete but in the notes I have given whatever recollection I have of where I found the verses. I would like to thank those individuals who entertained me with their verses and stories, including authors who embedded rhymes into their histories and memoirs.

I am particularly grateful to Gordon Williams, who ransacked his prodigious memory on my behalf and generously shared the treasures he found. He was an invaluable link to my parents and my past, and I was fortunate to have connected with him at the time of my early involvement with collecting rhymes. He died at the age of ninety-four, just as I was putting the finishing touches on this manuscript, and I very much miss finding his wonderful letters in my post box.

Tara Bryan of walking bird press supplied the decorative cast cuts that appear with the chapter headings. Many of these were originally used in Newfoundland and Labrador magazines and newspapers prior to the 1950s.

Finally, I would like to acknowledge the contribution of the late Elsie Murray, her husband P.J. Murray, and all her family. I never came away from a meal at Murray's Pond without having learned something that furthered my education as a Newfoundlander.

Hush Little Baby

1. Infant Verses

In Newfoundland and Labrador, very few nursery rhymes were really for the nursery. For one thing, there were few nurseries as such. Most families were large, like my own, and I shared a room with three older sisters and a baby brother until I was in my teens. Then one of the sisters left for school and the lucky boy was squeezed into a tiny room of his own. At least I didn't have to share a bed, although the house was so cold I often rented myself out to one of my siblings, who nicknamed me "The Furnace" and sometimes paid me as much as a dime to crawl in with them.

We had a few lullabies, one of which suggested the best way to deal with Mama's baby was to "Twist his neck and hit him on the head, / Throw him in a ditch and he'll be dead." Boo men and kidnappers, ghosts and evil fairies were more often conjured up to put rackety children to sleep than fairy godmothers or angels. The only angels we were aware of were the ones who came to take you away for good. My older sisters were taught by the nuns to sleep with their hands crossed on their breasts in case they died during the night, and the older sisters taught this to the babies, or at least tried to.

The truly joyful rhymes were for baby-bouncing games, where you were perched on the ankle of a crossed leg, and jounced up and down to imitate riding a horse. Sometimes you would be bounced on both knees, until a crow came and then down you would slip between the legs so as to almost-but-not-quite hit the floor. The grand old Duke of York marched up and down, the farmer rode his grey mare, the ladies trit-a-treed, and, if my brother John was in charge of the game, he usually didn't stop until baby had thrown up or threatened to with some conviction.

The usual English Mother Goose-style nursery rhymes that are known throughout the United States and Canada were well known in Newfoundland and Labrador, including "I Saw Esau," "Humpty Dumpty," "Little Boy Blue," "Pat-a-cake," and so on. We children also knew any number of authored verses, which served the same function as the anonymous nursery rhymes. Pope's "I Am His Highness' Dog at Kew," Brown's "I Do Not Love Thee, Dr. Fell," or Lear's "They dined on mince and slices of quince, / Which they ate with a runcible spoon" were as familiar as "Mussels in the Corner."

I have included here a few verses from the Aboriginal tradition. Rose Pamack made a small collection of infant rhymes in Inuktitut which I found in a manuscript at the Department of Indian and Northern Affairs some decades ago. She explained that each child had a special rhyme composed specifically for him or her, although sometimes the verses were borrowed from the English tradition and translated into the Aboriginal language. I recall, during a canoe trip on the Mista Shipu, listening to Bart Penashue singing his grandmother's hymns to his nephew while they lay together in a corner of the tent one sunny, sleepy afternoon.

The verses that follow are a grab bag of all sorts of the infant amusements I remembered or recorded, a sampler or smorgasbord of what is there to tempt a smile out of a tired, cranky, or bored toddler.

1. Bay boy, bay boy, come to your supper,
   Two cods' heads and a lump of butter.

2. Hush little baby,
   Lie down and be good,
   Before the old boo man
   Comes out of the wood,
   When he comes out,
   He'll have nothing to say
   Only wrap up the baby
   And take it away.

3. Go to bed, Tom,
   Go to bed, Tom,
   Put on the kettle
   And beat on the drum.

4. Go to sleep my dolly dear,
   Mama holds you, never fear.
   Little eyelids downward creep,
   Dolly soon will be asleep.

5. If you tell a lie,
   The boogie-man will get you,
   Your nose is gonna grow
   And everyone will know.

6. Jusualu, Daisilu,
   Imittasimajuuk,
   Qattakakulunga.
   Naaviniatluni
   Qajqajylummi
   Paallagumik.

7. Takseakujauvogalo emak
   Mariagolak
   Persikapuk
   Malleagolait
   Kangetegut
   Sajokaumejarlone.

8. One, two, three, four, five, six, seven,
   All good children go to heaven,
   All bad children stay below
   To keep in company with Old Black Joe.

9. Sleepy Susan goes to bed
   In the afternoon,
   Put a basin on her head
   Sucks a tablespoon.

10. Oh I'm the ghost of the breadcrust man,
    I scare young children whenever I can,
    I scare them all from one to another,
    Who do not eat breadcrusts and listen to mother.

11. Little Susan Dixon, don't you cry,
    Your mother is coming home by and by.

12. Bread and butter will make you stutter,
    Bread and cheese will make you sneeze,
    Pea soup will make you poop,
    Toast and tea will make you pee …

13. Barber, barber, shave a Mason,
    Chop off his head and put it in a basin,
    Four and twenty, that's enough,
    Give the barber a pinch of snuff.

14. Tiddley Winks the barber,
    Went to shave his father,
    The razor slipped and cut his lip,
    Tiddley Winks the barber.

Robin McGrath

15. Menton fourchu
    Bouche d'argent
    Nez pointu
    Joue rôtie
    Joue bouillie
    Tit-oeil
    Gros-t-oeil
    Poque! A la mailloche.

16. I must not throw upon the floor,
    The crust I cannot eat,
    For many a hungry little one
    Would think it quite a treat.
    'Tis willful waste brings woeful want
    And I may live to say,
    Oh, how I wish I had the bread
    Which once I threw away.

17. This is the way the ladies ride,
    Trit-a-tree, trit-a-tree,
    This is the way the ladies ride,
    Trit-a-trit-a-tree.
    This is the way the gentlemen ride,
    Gallop-a-trot, gallop-a-trot,
    This is the way the gentlemen ride,
    Gallop-a-gallop-a-trot.
    This is the way the farmer rides,
    Hobbledy-hoy, hobbledy-hoy,
    This is the way the farmer rides,
    Hobbledy-hobbledy-hoy.

18. A farmer was riding upon his grey mare,
    Bumpety, bumpety, bump.
    Beside sat his daughter so rosy and fair,
    Bumpety, bumpety, bump.
    Along came a crow
    And they all tumbled down,
    Bumpety, bumpety, bump.
    The mare lost his shoe and the farmer his crown,
    Bumpety, bumpety, bump.

19. Johnny Walker down the street,
    Say your prayers and go to sleep.
    If you don't he'll come to you.
    In the middle of the night and cry out BOO!

20. I'm a tidy little widow
    And I runs a candy store,
    I sells apples for a penny
    And my name is on the door,
    Peppermint knobs and chicken bones
    And bulls eyes by the score,
    I can always tell when I hears my bell,
    They are coming back for more.

21. How'd you like to be a baby girl?
    How'd you like to be a baby girl?
    Cheeks like roses, hair up in a curl,
    How'd you like to be a baby girl?
    When your mommy gives you a smacky smack,
    Sometimes here and sometimes on the back,
    And, oh my word, she knows the way to whack,
    How'd you like to be a baby girl?

22. Nin nan nitauasiminan,
    Nin nan nitauasiminan,
    Nishiuenimananan,
    Nin nan nitauasiminan,
    Nin nan nitauasiminan,
    Tshakanapatshu, shakamaue
    Kamatshu tapaskaiet nin
    nin sheuenimaut
    tshishauan.

23. Peik mistamin
    Nish uapamin,
    Nist tamat.
    Tshanapashu manteskues
    Tsjoiomepeshu tutu mak nika
    Tshikanipashu eku tshi eitut
    Katshijskutshimatsheut-
    shiuapit.

• • •

2. Les Harris recorded a parody of this or a similar verse: "Hush-a-bye-baby, / Your food's in a tin. / Mommy has got a nice sitter in. / Hush-a-bye-baby, / Now don't get a twinge / While Daddy and Mommy / Are out on a binge."

3. "Go to bed, Tom" was the nickname for the Warwickshire Regiment tattoo. The Opies recorded it as "Go to bed, Tom, / Go to bed, Tom, / Tired or not, Tom, / Go to bed, Tom." Other variants include "Get up

in the morning? And beat the big drum." This version came from the Southern Shore.

4. The verse "Go to Sleep My Dolly Dear" came from Bell Island.

6. "Jusualu, Dasilu" translates as "Joshua and Dorothy / Are going to fetch water, / Their little bucket / Tipped over and emptied / When they fell down / On the little hill."

7. "Takseakujauvogalo emak" is a song Judith Solomon used to sing to herself when her father put her to ride in the nose of his kayak. It translates as "Little Maria, sleeping on the tiny wave, when she's inside the kayak." I found it in Tim Borlase's *Songs of Labrador*, reprinted from *Them Days*.

8. Old Black Joe was the devil.

10. "The Breadcrust Man" was collected from Bishop's Cove by John Widdowson.

11. "Little Susan Dixon" is a rhyme from Labrador.

12. "Bread and Butter" is a game where children have to name a food and find a rhyme, the more scatological the better. Gordon Williams gave me these examples.

13. "Barber, Barber, Shave a Mason" is a face-washing game, a sectarian version of the old English rhyme "Barber, barber, shave a pig, / How many hairs to make a wig." This version comes from Brigus.

15. This verse is a baby rhyme identifying the features of the face: "Indented chin, / Mouth of silver / Pointed nose, / Cheek of toast, / Cheek of pap, / Little eye, / Big eye, / Poque! to the beetle." It is similar to the English rhyme "Here's the Lord Mayor." It was collected by Memorial University professor Gerald Thomas.

16. "I Must Not Throw upon the Floor" is a *Royal Reader* verse, but it

is so widely known and quoted to small children that it deserves to be included with the pre-school verses.

18. According to the Opies, this knee-bouncing rhyme dates back to at least 1805. It became popular after it was illustrated by Randolph Caldecott in 1884. Caldecott's version had slightly different words and a third verse about a mischievous raven.

19. We had a neighbour on Bonaventure Avenue named Johnny Walker, a very distinguished old gentleman, who bore a resemblance to the figure on the whiskey bottle, and I always thought it a great joke that anyone thought he would frighten me. In retrospect, I now wonder if his name really was Johnny Walker or if that was just a nickname we children gave him.

20. Peppermint knobs, chicken bones, and bulls eyes are all candies. Peppermint knobs and chicken bones are still made at the Purity factory in St. John's. Chicken bones are pink satin candy with chocolate marrow. Furey's made cod bones, white satin with peanut butter filling. Bulls eyes, or pulled molasses candies, resembled humbugs but were not successfully made commercially as they tended to go chalky after a day or so. They were made fresh by women in their homes and delivered to shops all around town by boys known as "bulls eye runners."

21. In "How'd You Like to Be a Baby Girl?," at "sometimes here" you hold out her hand, and at "sometimes on the back," you smack her backside. I was given this little song by Otto Tucker.

22. This Innu lullaby was sung by Jean Einish to her granddaughter and Matnen's daughter Manteskues also called Stephanie Pinette: "This is my baby, / This is my baby, / And I love this baby a lot. / This is my baby, / This is my baby, / And she's going to sleep / All night long, / Because I really love this child."

23. This is another lullaby composed for Manteskues: "One orange, / Two apples, / Three tomatoes, / And she goes to sleep / With Grandma and Grandpa / And she goes to school / In the morning when she gets up."

King George's Son

2. Games

When my children were small, my sister Janet told me to take lots of photographs because I wouldn't remember much otherwise, and she was absolutely right. I think sleep deprivation does that to you. The only games I can recall my kids playing—other than chess and Dungeons and Dragons—were "Rock, Paper, Scissors" and something called "Punchbuggy," which was played in the car and seemed to involve a lot of yelling and arguing.

From my own childhood I can remember dozens of games. There were outdoor games such as "Red Rover," "Hoist Your Sails and Run," "Red Light," and "Statues," as well as that old perennial, "Piddley," which was known elsewhere as "Cat Ball" or "Snig," and there were indoor ring games that were usually played at school. Ring games were really modified dances that involved song and ritualized slow movement, as distinct from outdoor games, which involved running, tagging, and hiding and seeking.

"King William Was King George's Son" is probably the best known of the Newfoundland and Labrador ring games. There was also "Ring around the Rosy," "London Bridge," "Go in and out the Windows," "The Big Ship Sails through the Illey Alley Oh," "Lazy Mary," and a dozen others.

Some outdoor games could be modified to be played indoors. Alleys were played with a mot outdoors, but with a ring on the linoleum or a pattern on a carpet indoors. Ball-bouncing games could be played in the front hall if Father wasn't home. Jacks could be played anywhere, and I distinctly remember my mother showing us how to play using six pebbles instead of the usual five commercial metal spikes and a ball—she must have been desperate to distract us from some threatened uprising. At a recent wedding, I watched as my great-nieces and great-nephews organized a game that seemed to be a combination of Red Light and Red Rover in the community hall where the supper was being laid out.

Another form of play that spilled over into the garden during the summer was amateur dramatics. Perhaps it was only in families as big as ours that these performances were done at home, but we did puppet plays, Christmas nativity plays, mock weddings, and, best of all, shadow surgery. Shadow surgery required only a bed sheet (white, as there was no other kind), a light source, and a variety of odds and ends such as scissors and butcher knives, bowls of cold spaghetti, and dead mice, and, of course, a corpse. There was also a funeral game called "Dead Baby."

Gary Saunders of Clarke's Head has written that girls and boys played different games, but, in my circle, everyone played just about everything, although as we got older the boys favoured shinny and the girls preferred skipping ropes. I gave up hockey after I accidentally blackened the eye of a boy I liked very much. The truth is that I was a rotten player and I was mortified by my own clumsiness. He was probably also better at skipping rope.

I was gratified, during a visit to my grandson's nursery school in Toronto, to discover that, with prompting, I remembered a lot of songs and actions that I must have learned when my own children were small. I was able to sing "The Wheels on the Bus" and "Mary Mack" along with all the Portuguese, Russian, and Italian mothers and grandmothers, so perhaps the parental amnesia my sister talked about is reversible in old age.

1. King William was King George's son,
   And all the royal races won,
   On his breast a star he wore
   Pointing to the Governor's door.
   Come choose to the east,
   Come choose to the west,
   Come choose the very one that you like best,
   If she's not there to take your part,
   Choose another with all your heart.
   Down on the carpet you must kneel,
   Just as the grass grows in the field,
   Kiss your true love, kiss her sweet,
   You may rise upon your feet.

2. The big ship sails through the Illey Alley Oh,
   The Illey Alley Oh, the Illey Alley Oh,
   The big ship sails through the Illey Alley Oh,
   On the nineteenth of September.

3. A duck and a drake
   And a saltwater cake,
   And a penny to pay the old baker,
   A hop and a scotch
   In another notch,
   Sletherum slatherum take her.

4. Red Rover, Red Rover,
   Send Adrian over.

5. One for sorrow,
   Two for joy,
   Three for a wedding,
   Four for a boy,
   Five for silver,
   Six for gold,
   Seven for a secret
   That will never be told.

6. Hide and seek all the week,
   All except for Sunday,
   Sunday is the holy day
   And so is Easter Monday.

7. Green gravel, green gravel,
   The grass is so green,
   And all the young maidens
   So fair to be seen,
   Oh Mary, oh Mary, your true love is dead,
   He sends you a letter to turn back your head.

8. I'll tell you the story
   Of Johnny Magory,
   Shall I begin it?
   That's all that's in it.
   I'll tell you another,
   About his brother,
   He had an awl
   And he nailed it to the wall
   And that's all.

9. Qau tungaya tungaya tungaya,
    Aqa suangalo itigat suangalo
    Aulat sanavit ingalat sanavit
    Qau tungaya tungaya tungaya.

10. Sailing in the boat 'til the tide runs high,
    Sailing in the boat 'til the collar flags fly,
    Sailing in the boat 'til the tide runs high,
    Waiting for the pretty girls to come by and by.
    Choose your partner now today,
    Choose, oh choose her right away,
    I don't care what the old folks say.
    Oh what a horrible choice you've made,
    And she can no longer stay.
    Since she can no longer stay,
    Give her a kiss and send her away.

11. Have a cup of tea, sir?
    No, sir. Why, sir?
    'Cause I got a cold, sir,
    Down the North Pole, sir.
    What ya doing there, sir?
    Catching a polar bear, sir.

12. Bless the Regatta that brought us together,
    Big men and little men, short men and tall,
    Some from the seaside and some from the heather,
    Citymen, countrymen, but oarsmen all.

13. Heigh ho, wherever you're at,
    Don't show the brim of your hat:
    Hoist your sails and run!

14. Charlie Chaplin went to France
    To get a patch put on his pants,
    The patch was small and that is all,
    So I gave Charlie a rubber ball.

15. Erin's in the kitchen,
    Doin' a bit of stitchin',
    In comes Liam
    And pushes her OUT!

16. One, two, three,
    Out goes she!

• • •

1. "King William Was King George's Son" is a ring game or dance, as well known in Kentucky and Virginia as in Newfoundland and Labrador. When my father was studying public health in Kentucky in the 1930s, he used to go to the hill dances with John Jacob Niles, and he told us that many of the songs and ballads he heard were the same ones we knew at home. One of the American variants of this verse is "On his breast he wore a star / To show the world he was a man of war," which perhaps reflects the American view of England after the Revolution.

2. "The Big Ship Sails" is a ring dance or game, also known in Ireland and England. "The Illey Alley Oh" is the name Irish children gave to the sea. Sandra Cooze records it as the "holly holly, ho."

3. To play "Ducks and Drakes" is to skip stones on the water.

4. "Red Rover" involves two teams, one linking hands to form a barrier which a player from the other side must try to break. If the runner fails to break through, he or she must join that side. The runner aims for the weakest link, so success depends on the strategic placement of your strongest players next to your weakest ones.

5. "One for Sorrow" is a way to predict the future by counting the number of crows that fly by.

7. "Green Gravel" is a ring game, so the verse is sung. Fearon and Fritz record it as "Oh Mary, oh Mary, / Your true love is here, / I'll send you a ribbon / To tie back your hair," which I suspect is a bowdlerization of the original, which the Opies report was recorded in Manchester, England, as early as 1835.

8. Johnny Magory (a rose hip) appears in many children's rhymes. This one is told as a teasing game with a child who wants a story. "The Seige of Bell Isle," listed elsewhere in this volume, is a similarly short, endless non-story.

9. "Qau tungaya" is a song from Nain, sung by children while playing they are hunting whales.

10. "Sailing in the Boat" is a ring game (a "collar flag" is a tie). I found numerous variations of this song, but the one I've chosen came from Otto Tucker.

11. "Have a Cup of Tea, Sir?" is one of several verses I was given by Mary Niamh McGettigan of Harbour Main.

12. From Jack Fitzgerald's *A Day at the Races*.

13. "Hoist Your Sails and Run" was a hide-and-seek game. I grew up believing that this was a game about illegal settlers running away from British gunboats. Variants identified by Fearon and Fritz include "High low, lie low, / Don't show / The brim of your hat / Wherever you're at," "Lie flat where you're at / And don't show the bill of your hat," and "Keep low, keep in, / Don't show the hair of your chin." At the cry "Hoist your sails and run," you would pull the skirt of your jacket or coat up over your head to make a sail, and run. Swilers at the ice would "sail" a pan of ice in a similar way.

14. "Charlie Chaplin" is a ball-bouncing rhyme.

15. "Erin's in the Kitchen" is a skipping rhyme. A second skipper runs in and pushes the first clear on the beat of "OUT!" Obviously, it takes cooperation to carry out the elimination successfully.

Four Legs Up Cold as Stone

3. Riddles

"As I Was Walking on London Bridge" is the first riddle I remember hearing when I was a child, a riddle that in its original incarnation ran, "A stick in his hand, a stone in his throat / Tell me the answer and I'll give you a groat." I could not guess the answer and could not fathom how others could, no matter how long they wracked their brains over it. Recently, I got the same reaction from some students in Labrador. A young man in the class, genuinely trying to puzzle through the attraction of riddles for our ancestors, declared that to untangle a riddle, he'd have to be stuck in a snowbank in a storm for three days with no gas for his skidoo.

I think he hit the nail on the head. Our grandparents had long days, dark nights, and uninterrupted, repetitive work such as knitting nets and spinning wool that allowed them the mental leisure to work out these tricky brainteasers.

Clarence and Sarah Dewling, writing about the 1930s outports, claimed that the riddle process was a social convention, a diversion of sorts for the children present. They believed the riddles were always well known to the adults, as were the answers, and the participants were careful not to show off by asking an unknown riddle or by providing the answer to a known one. It was the riddler's job to reveal the answer if a child did not guess it. I believe they are right about this as I frequently heard the same riddles repeated many times, and I don't recall people jumping in with the answer.

People are often able to remember riddles without knowing the answers (I still haven't found the answer to one of the riddles I present here), so obviously the rhyme helps the riddle stick in the brain. According to Iona and Peter Opie, the Elizabethan age was "the hey-day of the rhyming riddles," and one of the oldest of the riddles I found—the one that begins "Cut off my head and singular I act"—is from that era. Riddles are no longer as popular as they were in Shakespeare's time, but when I went looking for them, a surprising number of people were able to recall at least one.

It is no coincidence that both Mary Dalton and Tom Dawe, Newfoundland's two great poets, have given riddles a central place in their work. What is a poetic metaphor but a riddle? A good riddle has the same staying power as a poem—you can hear it over and over and still appreciate the clever way it has been pieced together.

> 1. As I was walking on London Bridge,
>   I met a man with a red hat,
>   A stick in his hand, a stone in his belly—
>   Tell me the answer and I'll give you a penny.

> 2. Cut off my head and singular I act,
>   Cut off my tail and plural I appear,
>   Cut off my head and tail and wondrous fact,
>   Although my middle's left, there's nothing there.
>   What is my head cut off? A sounding sea.
>   What is my tail cut off? A flowing river
>   In whose translucent depths I fearless play,
>   Parents of sweetest sound yet mute forever.

> 3. Flour from Scotland, raisins from Spain,
>   Mixed together in a shower of rain,
>   A calico bag and a reeving string,
>   Tell me the riddle and I'll give you a ring.

> 4. Poulous en hors,
>   Pouloux en d'dans,
>   Leve la jambe
>   Et fourre dedams?

> 5. Adam and Eve and Pinch Me
>   Went down to the river to bathe,
>   Adam and Eve fell in,
>   Who do you think was saved?

6. In I went, out I came,
   I saw life where death had been
   Six caught fast, seventh went free
   Riddle me this or hung I'll be.

7. It's love I sit, and love I feel,
   It's love I hold steadfast in my hand,
   I can see love but love can't see me,
   Riddle me this or hung I'll be.

8. Four legs up cold as stone,
   Two legs down flesh and bone,
   The head of the living in the mouth of the dead
   Tell me the riddle and I'll go to bed.

9. Forty weeks of anticipation,
   Ten of hustling preparation,
   One to pack and reach the station,
   One of final realization.

10. As I was going to St. Ives,
    I met a man with seven wives,
    And every wife had seven sacks
    And every sack had seven cats,
    And every cat had seven kits,
    Kits, cats, sacks and wives,
    How many were going to St. Ives?

11. 'Tis nothing much at first,
    A gleam, a tiny spark
    That glows, half flickers out,
    And yet drives back the dark.

12. Long legs and crooked thighs,
    Little head and no eyes.

13. Elizabeth, Betsy and Bess,
    Went over the hill to find a bird's nest,
    They found a nest with three eggs in it,
    They took one apiece—how many were left?

14. Full of legs, raggedy jags,
    Stands still and never wags.

15. Big at the bottom,
    Little at the top,
    A tongue in the middle
    That goes flippety flop.

16. Long and slender like a trout,
    When he bawls his guts come out.

17. In the meadow runs a deer,
    With golden horns and golden hair.
    Neither fish, flesh, feathers nor bone,
    But in the meadow he runs alone.

18. When people's sick they come to me,
    I physics, bleeds and sweats 'em,
    Sometimes they live, sometimes they die—
    What's that to me? I lets 'em.

19. I washed in a water
    Never rained nor flowed,
    Dried my face in a napkin
    Never spun nor sewed.

20. Take a great poet of another day,
    Strike off a great weight and add a "k."
    Of another great poet, 5 letters I think,
    Stick on behind to make a popular drink.

21. Two Ns, two Os, an L and a D,
    Put them together and spell it for me.

22. Pray tell us ladies, if you can,
    Who is that highly favoured man
    Who though he has married many a wife
    May be a bachelor all his life.

23. Through a rock, through a reel,
    Through an old spinning wheel,
    Through a hopper, through a lopper,
    Through an old bowl of copper,
    Through an old cow's shinbone,
    Though its heart was never known.

24. Four stiff standers,
    Four dilly danders,
    Two lookers,
    Two crookers
    And a wig wag.

25. Here's to the happiest days of me life,
    Spent in the arms of another man's wife.

26. Oh Mary Mack, Mack, Mack,
    All dressed in black, black, black,
    With silver buttons, buttons, buttons,
    All down her back, back, back.

27. Riddle me, riddle me, riddle me right,
    Where was I last Saturday night?
    The winds did blow and the trees did shake,
    I saw a hole the fox did make.

28. Sisters and brothers have I none
    But this man's father is my father's son.

29. Port and starboard,
    Forward and aft,
    Inside on both sides
    On every craft.

30. The wind was West
    And West steered we,
    With all sails full—
    How could that be?

• • •

1. A cherry. This riddle came from Mrs. Marie (Tiny) Janes. The "groat" of the earlier version was either a silver coin issued in England until 1662, or more likely a fourpenny piece issued between 1836 and 1856.

2. Cod: "od" for odd, unusual; "co" for company; "o" or nothing; "c" or sea; "d" for the river Dee.

3. A pudding in a bag. Alternatively it is "Flour of England, fruit of Spain, / Mix it together in a shower of rain, / Put it in a bag, tie it with a string, / Tell me the riddle and I'll give you a ring." The Opies document speculation that it might have referred to the proposed marriage of Queen Mary of England and Phillip II of Spain. This version comes from Clarence and Sarah Dewling of Trouty.

4. Un bas de laine, or "Hairy out, / Hairy in, / Lift your leg / And stick it in"—a stocking. This riddle comes from the west coast of Newfoundland, which is perhaps why the French is a bit unusual. From Gerald Thomas's "Etudes de folklore et d'histoire orale chez les franco-terreneuvienas," in *Folklore and Oral History*, edited by Neil Rosenberg.

5. The answer is "Pinch Me," and the person gets pinched when he or she answers.

6. I initially thought this riddle had something to do with graves and maggots, but Les Harris records a variant about a bird's nest inside a skull, with six of seven eggs already hatched: "Six there were, seven there'll be / Riddle me this and I'll go free." John Widdowson records a variant regarding a bird nesting in the carcass of a horse: "As I was walking down the lane, / Out of the dead the living came."

7. According to my cousin Anna Guigné, a little crackie named Love died, and his owner made a chair of his bones. Les Harris records a variation which is about a chair made from the bones of a murdered sweetheart.

8. A man walking with a bark pot on his head. This riddle appears in Nellie Strowbridge's novel *Far From Home*.

9. A vacation. I believe this riddle was made up by my aunt, Elizabeth McGrath Conroy [Mennie]. It appeared in *Inter Nos*, the Mercy College annual.

10. One—the riddler. The others are coming from St. Ives. The Opies say this well-known English riddle, which my father used to tell, is at least 250 years old. There is a more complex version that includes lice and mice and the time of day, but this is the only version I recall hearing.

11. A candle. This little verse was written by Leslie Pardy and was originally published in *Them Days*.

12. Tongs. This riddle appears with "short thighs" in the early 1800s, and the "crooked" version is first documented in England in 1842. This one was recorded by R.F. Sparkes in *The Winds Softly Sigh*.

13. Two, as Elizabeth, Betsy, and Bess are all the same girl. According to the Opies, who were writing in 1950, the riddle is "of a style common in the seventeenth century, and has been consistently popular during the past hundred years." This version came from Gordon Williams.

14. A fish flake. The verse is found in the *Dictionary of Newfoundland English*.

15. A bell. The Opies recorded also "As round as an apple, / As deep as a pail, / It never cries out / Till it's caught by the tail" (a bell) and "As round as an apple, / As deep as a cup, / And all the king's horses / Cannot pull it up" (a well).

16. A gun. My sister Janet Kelly told me this riddle.

17. The sun shining on a brook. This riddle comes from Englee.

18. Dr. I. Lettsome.

19. Dew on grass. This Salvage riddle comes from Fred Olford, recorded by Robert Finch in *The Iambics of Newfoundland*.

20. Milkshake: Milton, minus a "ton," plus "k," plus Shakespeare minus five letters (or perhaps six). This riddle was created by the mathematician Dr. Albert (Tommy) Wilansky when he was a boy and published in his newspaper *The Familydom*.

21. London or "it." This riddle was a favourite of my grandfather, George Kearney, and was handed on from him to my uncle Gerard Kearney, and from Uncle Gerry to his daughter Anna Guigné, who gave it to me.

22. A clergyman. This riddle was printed on a china plate in a house at Coley's Point.

23. "Through a rock, through a reel" has the earmarks of a riddle, but nobody I spoke to had an answer for it. Then I found that Les Harris records a version which includes "an old tin dipper" and other items, and ends, "Was there ever such a riddle, / Since the world was known?" The answer was "a beetle."

24. "Four stiff standers" is a cow, and you can mime the cow using your fingers to make the legs, udders, horns, and eyes. I remember this riddle from my very early years. The Opies report that it is known throughout Europe, one variant from 1820 being: "Two lookers, two crookers, / Four hangers, four gangers, / And a flap to scare the flies away."

25. "Another man's wife" is "Mudder."

26. "Mary Mack" is a coffin. This riddle is now a song, popular in nursery schools, and a variation has also been recorded by Great Big Sea. In Toronto, it is paired with another rhyme that we considered a completely separate entity: "I asked my mother for fifty cents, / To see the elephant jump the fence." This verse had a variety of rude endings, and doesn't seem in any way related to the original "Mary Mack."

27. From a folktale about a man digging a grave for his sweetheart, recorded by John Widdowson in *Folk Speech*, Book I, p. 16.

28. A man introducing his son.

29. Lanyard knots, as recorded by Les Harris.

30. "The Wind Was West" is about a helmsman whose name was West. From Les Harris, *Growing Up with Verse*.

Cry Baby Cry

4. Teases and Taunts

Children are often cruel to one another, and, while we pay lip service to the fact that "Sticks and stones will break my bones, / But names will never hurt me," we all learned early on that it isn't true. Names and taunts and smart-aleck remarks can cut to the bone and stay with you all your life. I was lucky. The name Robin always elicits "the big, fat bobbin," which I often heard, but, since at that time there wasn't enough flesh on me to bait a hook, it didn't hurt. Had I been a pudgy child, it would have been torment.

Two of the more common insults of my childhood were, in retrospect, somewhat puzzling. The first was "Go home, your mother's baking buns," and the second was "Hey, you with the hair like mine ... mine's like a tar brush!" These taunts are rather benign by today's standards, but you had to look out because the words were often followed by a well-directed rock. Being a rather sensitive infant, overly inclined to tears, I was more likely to have "Ya big sook!" hurled at me. There was not much point trying to make someone cry when they were already bawling their eyes out.

Old habits die hard and the fine art of the childhood insult was often honed and refined in the forge of adult life, examples of which can be found in the selection of political rhymes. These "quisms" often have impenetrable origins. For example, "He's got the face of a robber's horse," meaning he has a lot of gall, has been explained to me as suggesting he's a horse's ass, since the robber is riding away, or because the robber rides backwards on his horse. However, the Opies have a quite different explanation for the idea that "the horse's head's where his tail should be," as can be seen in the chapter on animal verses.

The meanings of some of these insults escape me to this day, though I have heard them many times. I know what's meant when someone says

"I wouldn't spit down his throat if he were dying of thirst," but not if they say "If there were two hens in the woods, he'd be one of them." I was recently lamenting that today most people just resort to the tiresome four-letter words, when there is great poetry in the art of the insult, and a come-from-away assured me that I have a jaded ear and the fine art of the insult is alive and well in Newfoundland and Labrador.

1. Shut up your mouth,
   Your tongue is hanging out,
   Put it in a tea can
   And never let it out.

2. Giddy giddy gout,
   With your shirt tail out,
   Five yards in
   And six yards out.

3. They laughed at Ma,
   They screamed at Pa,
   When we went to Topsail
   In our first motor car.

4. All big policemen
   Got flat feet;
   Pit-a-pat, pit-a-pat,
   Down Water Street.

5. Dirty Lil, Dirty Lil,
   Lives on top of Flower Hill,
   Never washes, never will,
   Huck-ptooey! Dirty Lil.

6. Up and down the Southern Shore
   Sometime after supper,
   See this great big ugly thing
   Go after Charlie Tucker.

7. I'm Kay Whelan from the bay,
   I'm as ugly as they say,
   It's not fair, but I don't care,
   'Cause I'm Kay Whelan from the bay.

8. If you want to marry a girl,
   Marry a Newfoundlander,
   If you want to marry a fool,
   Marry a Scotch Highlander.

9. Fifty pence
   Up on the fence,
   Colliers' people
   Got no sense.

10. G'wan home, your mudder is callin'
    Your father just fell in the garbage can,
    G'wan home, your mudder is callin',
    They've come to collect your drunken old man.

11. Spoons, forks, cups and knives,
    Her Yankee father had two wives.

12. Robin McGrath is no good,
    Chop her up for firewood.
    When she's dead,
    Cut off her head,
    And bake her up in gingerbread.

13. What's in the pot
    With the cover half squat!

14. Guts for garters,
    That's for starters.

15. See my finger?
    See my thumb?
    See my fist?
    You'd better run!

16. Step on a crack,
    Break your mother's back.

17. Torbay b'ys is gone to the woods,
    And you know that they are rindin',
    Gunny sacks upon their backs
    And their grub-bags streeled behind 'em.
    Up the street as thick as flies
    Dirty necks and dirty ties,
    Dirty rings around their eyes,
    Dirty old Torbay men.

    Ask the bayman for a chew,
    He's afraid you might take two,
    Bites it off to give to you,
    Dirty Newfoundlander.
    Ask the bayman for a smoke,
    He will say his pipe is broke,
    On that smoke I hope he choke,
    Dirty Newfoundlander.

18. April Fool is gone and past
    You're the biggest fool at last
    Up a ladder down a tree,
    You're a bigger fool than me.
    Skin a chicken, skin a hen,
    You're a bigger fool again.

19. Come day, go day,
    God send Sunday.

20. Red, red, piss-a-bed,
    Five cents a cabbage head.

21. Little Dickie Doubt,
    Is your mother out,
    With your hands in your pockets
    And your shirttail out?

22. Roses are red,
    Violets are bluish,
    With a name like that
    You must be Jewish.

23. Protestant, Protestant, ring the bell
    To call the devil out of hell!

24. Catholic, Catholic, go to mass,
    Riding on the devil's ass.

25. Horse and buggy, horse and buggy,
    Horse and buggy team,
    The Goulds got the horse and buggy
    The Harbour got the steam.

26. Blueberries are blueberries,
    Cactus are cactus,
    The Harbour plays the Goulds
    Just for practice.

27. The down-the-bayers set their traps
    So early in the fall,
    Their hunt is large in number
    While ours are very small.
    Half the fur they get are stag
    While ours are all prime—
    I would not give a skin of mine,
    No, not for eight or nine.

28. All the jailers are nearly wild,
     Their grief is awful sad,
     Because they lost their darling boy,
     Their little English lad.

29. A moment on the lips,
     A lifetime on the hips.

30. Your claws will never
     maintain your jaws.

31. Scaredy cat
     To kill a rat.

32. Salvation Army,
     Make the devil run,
     Running down the stockpile
     Up to Number One.

33. Johnny in the woodpile,
     Johnny on the fence,
     Johnny got his haircut
     For fifty-five cents,
     I told Ma,
     Ma told Pa,
     Johnny got a lickin',
     Ha, ha, ha.

34. James is mad and I am glad,
     And I know how to tease him.
     Give him a drink to make him think,
     And Lizabeth Anne to squeeze him.

35. Trick or treat, smell my feet,
     Give me something good to eat,
     Not too big, not too small
     Just as big as Montreal.

36. Silas and Tyler were fighting for flies,
    Silas gave Tyler a pair of black eyes,
    Caleb the baby he started to roar,
    Now, said Kathryn, don't fight any more.

37. Taffy was a Welshman,
    Taffy was a thief,
    Taffy came to my house
    And stole a pound of beef,
    I went to Taffy's house,
    Taffy wasn't there,
    Taffy came to my house
    And stole a case of beer,
    I went to Taffy's house,
    Taffy wasn't in,
    Taffy came to my house
    And stole a pint of gin,
    I went to Taffy's house,
    Taffy was in bed,
    I took the empty bottle
    And I hit him on the head.

38. A kitchen and a porchful,
    And I can't get a cupful.

39. Poor Jack-o-lantern,
    He's not doing well,
    He's too bad for Heaven
    And too good for Hell.

40. Old Mother Witch
    Couldn't sew a stitch,
    Picked up a penny
    And thought she was rich.

41. The parson was poor
    And so were the people
    So they sold the bells
    To repair the steeple.

42. Holy Moses, king of the Jews,
    Sold his wife for a pair of shoes.
    When the shoes began to wear,
    Holy Moses began to swear.
    When the swearing began to stop,
    Holy Moses bought a shop.
    When the shop began to sell,
    Holy Moses went to hell.

•••

1. Said to a talkative person.

3. Recorded by Arthur Priestman Cameron in the *Newfoundland Quarterly* (Fall 1987), with regard to R.G. Reid importing the first car into Newfoundland.

4. "All Big Policemen" is usually accompanied by hands being drummed on the ground.

8. This insult to Highlanders came from Helen Fogwill Porter.

11. "Spoons, forks, cups and knives" came from M.T. Dohaney's *A Fit Month for Dying*, and the first book of Dohaney's trilogy, *The Corrigan Women*.

13. This is the answer when someone says "What?"

14. I associate "Guts for Garters" with the Irish Christian Brothers, like the threat to "have your balls for bookends." However, in *The Newfoundland Tongue*, Nellie Strowbridge suggests it means "He'll take whatever he can get from me for his own use," in which case it belongs with the insults rather than the threats.

15. This threat is accompanied by a gesture, where the threatener gives the victim to the count of three by holding up a finger, a thumb, and then a fist before pummelling him or her senseless.

17. "The Dirty Old Torbay Man" has a variety of manifestations. Sometimes he's a "dirty Tory bayman," and sometimes he's a dance tune, sung to "Mussels in the Corner." The dirty faces come from honest hard labour, rindin' or taking the rinds or bark off trees in the woods. Rinds were used to cover salt fish and to roof tilts, so they were often saved. The men used to burn the brush to prevent bush fires and, in some seasons, to keep off the flies, so their faces became sooty. The "Dirty Newfoundlander" is a variation that is said to have originated in Argentia among the American servicemen.

18. April Fool only goes until noon on April 1, so, if someone tries a trick in the afternoon, they are said to be the biggest fool.

19. "Come day, go day" is said of, and to, a lazy person.

20. "Red, red" was said to a red-headed person.

22. Sometimes it's "With a nose like that / You must be Jewish."

23-24. "Protestant, Protestant" and "Catholic, Catholic" were recorded by Charles Hodgins, padre of the Newfoundland Regiment.

25. In "Horse and Buggy," the Harbour is Petty Harbour, possibly also a reference to their electric power plant.

27. The "Down-the-bayers" verse came from Max Blake of Rigolet.

28. The "little English lad" was Phil Brady, a convict who escaped from the Penitentiary in 1909.

30. This insult means you will always eat more than you will earn.

32. "Salvation Army, Make the Devil Run" refers to the stockpile and Number One Mine on Bell Island, but it sometimes ends "Going down Water Street / With the big base drum," or "Going up Gower Street, / Up to Number One." Number One was the New Gower Street Congregation Barracks.

37. According to the Opies, this song was used to taunt the Welsh on March 1, St. David's or St. Taffy's Day. In a 1780 version, Taffy steals a marrow bone and it concludes, "I went to Taffy's home / Taffy was in bed, / I took the marrow bone / And beat about his head." The only Welshman we knew was a local dentist who was thought to be tough on children, so we took some pleasure in reciting the Taffy verses.

38. "When there is a lot of company, the person living in the house has

to settle for little," according to Nellie Strowbridge in *The Newfoundland Tongue*.

39. From Helen Fogwill Porter in the *Globe and Mail*, October 21, 2006.

40. From Helen Fogwill Porter, quoted in Barbara Rieti's *Making Witches*.

41. From *Folk Speech*, Book I, by John Widdowson.

42. I don't recall this verse being aimed at Jews particularly—it was more an excuse to say "hell," which was a forbidden swear word.

I Met You as a Stranger

5. Friendship Books

About ten years ago, I received a note from a stranger, commenting on an article I had written for the St. John's *Telegram*. I can't remember what the article was about, but towards the end of the letter, my mystery correspondent asked if I was related to Jim McGrath who practiced medicine in St. Mary's Bay back in the thirties. Thus began a decade of correspondence, which continued until this year.

Every few weeks, I received a letter from Gordon Williams of Westbank, British Columbia, formerly of St. John's. Sometimes he included clippings from his local paper, often he had a verse or a joke to share with me, always he had some positive advice or some inspiring anecdote to pass on. Mr. Williams was well into his eighties when he began writing to me, but whether he was observing black bears in his garden, watching the construction of a huge new flyover bridge near his home, or celebrating a birthday or other holiday with his daughter or one of his grandchildren, he was living life to the fullest.

Gordon Williams and I never met, but I considered him one of my great friends, and I hope he would have said the same of me. When I began collecting Newfoundland and Labrador rhymes with a view to publishing an article or two about them, he was one of my best sources of new verses and rhymes, particularly those from friendship books.

Back in 'them' days, everyone had a friendship book. I had one, though goodness knows what happened to it, and you can still buy them in the dollar stores, but Gordon Williams still had his from his school days, and his daughter Elizabeth Corrigan still had hers. What's more, although Mr. Williams no longer had the actual book, his prodigious memory had retained some of the verses from his mother's album. The verses he sent me had been transmitted orally over a span of more than a century.

As he explained, the friendship book verses that were written by friends of the same sex were often sentimental, but nobody looked askance on them at that time. However, the friendship or autograph book was sometimes an opportunity for an acquaintance to forge a stronger bond with the owner, as was the case with the verse that opens this collection. It comes from Gordon Williams's autograph book and was written in there by Alice Bradbury, whose father was principal of the school in Heart's Content. Gordon and Alice later married and lived fifty-two happy years together until her death.

1. I met you as a stranger,
   I cannot part as such,
   For I have learned to like you—
   Can you say as much?

2. Think of me when you are happy.
   Keep for me one little spot
   In the depths of your affection,
   Plant a sweet forget-me-not.

3. Remember me now, remember me ever,
   Remember the night we slept together,
   You had the bed and all the clothes,
   I had the floor and nearly froze.

4. I oughta sing, I oughta laugh,
   But in your book, I autograph.

5. My pen is bad, my ink the same
   Only for that I would sign my name.

6. Many will write "forget-me-not"
   Upon these pages fair,
   But I will change the words and say
   "Forget me if you dare."

7. Every wish a friend can wish,
   My friend I wish for you.
   May you be happy while you live,
   Your trials brief and few.

8. Remembrance is the silken tie
   That binds two hearts together,
   And if we do not break that tie,
   Then we'll be friends forever.

9. Black is the raven,
   Black is the rook,
   But blacker the person
   Who steals this book.

10. You asked me for something original,
    But I hardly know how to begin,
    For there's nothing original in me,
    Not even original sin.

11. When you get old and give up hope,
    I'll wash your feet with Sunlight soap.

12. When you are far away,
    And your friend you cannot see,
    When in some chapel you are praying,
    Will you sometimes pray for me?

13. If writing in notebooks
    True friendship ensures,
    With the greatest of pleasure
    I'll scribble in yours.

14. What, write in your album for others to spy,
    And learned ones to laugh at? No, not I.

15. If there's room for me in your album,
    There's room for me in your heart;
    There's room for us both in heaven
    Where loved ones never part.

16. When your cat runs up a tree,
    Fetch it down and think of me.

17. As you go through life,
    Make this your goal—
    Watch the doughnut
    Not the hole.

18. When evening draws the curtains o'er
And pins them with a star,
Remember that you have a friend
Although she may be far.

19. When you get old and cannot see,
I'll hold the pot for you to pee.

20. Like a piece of driftwood on the sea,
May you never be alone like me.

21. Around went your book, and thither it came,
I ain't much of a poet, but here goes my name.

22. By hook or by crook,
I'll be last in your book.

23. My book and my heart
Will never part.

24. Be it ever so narrow,
You can write on the farrow.

•••

1. Friendship or autograph books originated in Germany in the sixteenth century and were brought to North America by German immigrant families in the 1850s. By the 1900s, the autograph book had become a children's custom and lighter, humorous verses and jokes became more common than the serious comments and quotations that had appeared previously. Friendship albums were usually circulated, so one had to be careful that rude rhymes didn't go in. Sometimes something like the following might sneak by a vigilant parent: "Many albums have I seen, / Some were red and others green, / But in Africa, where I have been, / All bums are black."

2. The forget-me-not has a particular resonance in Newfoundland as it was the flower used for remembering the fallen soldiers of the First

World War, before the introduction of the poppy. It is still worn by many on the anniversary of the July Drive.

3. Collected from Valerie Whelan of La Scie when we were attending Selma Barkham's Red Bay conference at Plum Point. This verse exhibits the double entendre that is typical of friendship book entries—suggesting an awareness of adult interests but confirming the innocence of friendship.

5. From Gordon Williams.

6. From Gordon Williams.

7. From Gordon Williams.

8. From Gordon Williams.

19. From Valerie Whelan of La Scie.

21. From Gordon Williams.

22. In a desperate attempt to stand out from all the others who have signed their names, it often became something of a competition to be at the very end of the friendship album.

23. This is an alphabet book rhyme, quoted in Barbara Rieti's *Making Witches*.

24. The farrow or "farl" is the cover of the book, and writing on the cover one-upped the person who wrote in the bottom corner of the last page. This example comes from the *Dictionary of Newfoundland English*.

Multiplication Is Vexation

6. School Rhymes

In the first decade after Confederation, it was still common to see vestiges of the old regime in Newfoundland and Labrador. Newfoundland stamps, hidden away in dusty desk drawers, would sometimes appear on packages, and Newfoundland coins would turn up in your change. If you got one of those tiny silver nickels, you might save it for Sunday to put in the collection plate where it almost passed for a dime. If you were really lucky and got a twenty-cent coin, you tried to spend it in a vending machine, where it was accepted as a quarter.

Newfoundland school books were also from the old curriculum, and I considered myself particularly lucky to have gone to a small school where the old textbooks were recycled far beyond their useful lives in the larger, more modern schools. We had all the *Royal Readers*, Cochrane's history text *The Story of Newfoundland*, Frances Briffett's *More Stories of Newfoundland*, and, from Wheaton's Educational Publishers in Exeter, England, Miss Edith Manuel's *Newfoundland Geography*, which in 1952 was revised and renamed *Newfoundland, Our Province*.

In town, students wore uniforms, while out around the bay they carried birch billets tied to their schoolbags to heat the schoolhouse, and in both places the schools were almost all denominational. In fact, our school days weren't much different from those of our parents or our grandparents. The strap was employed to keep discipline, more or less according to the whim and the stomach of the teacher, and nobody lost sleep at night worrying about the students' fragile egos. If you didn't pass the tests, you failed and repeated the grade. I had personal experience of that particular humiliation.

Then, as now, students felt powerless in the grip of the mandatory education system and one of the few ways they could strike back was with rhymes.

Probably the most widely known was the rhyme for the twenty-fourth of May holiday. Surprisingly, at least some of the rhymes were intended not so much to accuse the teachers of being brutal or hateful but to show how clever the children were.

1. While other girls wear miniskirts
   And go with boys—the little flirts—
   Or gloat about their gorgeous looks,
   I just sit and read my books.

2. Now I lay me down to sleep,
   A pile of homework at my feet,
   If I should die before I wake,
   Three requests I'd like to make:
   Lay my math book on my chest,
   Tell Mr. Mercer I did my best;
   Lay my history book at my feet,
   Tell Mr. Hiscock I got it beat;
   Lay my French book at my side,
   Tell Mr. Denny I'm glad I died.

3. Strap, strap, strap,
   On my cold bare hands! Oh gee!
   And I would that my tongue could utter
   The thoughts that arise in me.
   Oh well for the fisherman's boy
   That he takes it like a child at play,
   Oh well for the teacher's pet,
   That he keeps his tongue still all day,
   And the daily routine goes on
   And my tongue can never keep still,
   But oh for the day when my knuckles
   Shall lay the old bastard still.
   Strap, strap, strap,
   If it's pleasure for this get ye,
   But you shall regret every licking
   That you delivered to me.

4. We are brave, we are bold,
   When there's whiskey to be sold,
   In the cellars of St. Patrick's school,
   Run, run, run, I think I hear a nun,
   Pick up your whiskey and run.
   If Father Bradshaw should appear,
   Tell him it's spruce beer,
   In the cellars of St. Patrick's school.

5. In chemistry I'm doing well,
   The teacher says I'm fine,
   I'm sure I know where Carbon ate,
   But where did Iodine?

6. The reason we all study botany
   Is to see if we've brains or not any.

7. Joy to the world, the teacher's dead,
   We cut off her head,
   What happened to her body,
   We flushed it down the potty,
   And round and round it goes,
   And round and round it gocs,
   And round, and round, and round it goes.

8. You may travel from ocean to ocean,
   You may travel from sea to sea,
   But you'll never find a finer bunch,
   Than the boys of B.F.C.

9. Where we go to school each day,
   Indian children used to play:
   All about our native land
   Where the shops and houses stand.

10. Multiplication is vexation,
    Division is as bad,
    The Rule of Three does puzzle me
    And practice drives me mad.

11. Who is grammar?
    I say, damn her.

12. Latin is a language,
    As dead as dead can be,
    It killed the ancient Romans
    And now it's killing me.

13. Ann met an ant and an ant met Ann,
    "Hallo," said Ann. "Hallo, little man."
    Boys' boots are big and when boys jump,
    Boys' big boots go bump, bump, bump.
    Come, come cushy cow, come when I call,
    Come, come cushy cow, come to your stall.
    Dance, Dan, dance do
    Down the dale, I'll dance too.
    Eggs, eggs, new laid eggs, laid by my hen,
    Any fresh eggs, Ethel? Yes, Madam, ten ...

14. D is for disappointment, which we try not to do,
    O is for others, like me and like you,
    R is for races, which we run in May,
    M is for mothers, who are far, far away,
    I is for imagine, which we sometimes do,
    T is for tenderness, that is true,
    O is for office, which our teacher has here,
    R is for rest, we have our share,
    Y is for yes, which we answer with care.

15. St. Bon's boys are handsome,
    St. Pat's boys are smart,
    But it takes a boy from Holy Cross,
    To win a young girl's heart.

16. The twenty-fourth of May
    Is the Queen's birthday,
    If we don't get a holiday
    We'll all run away.
    Kick up tables, kick up chairs,
    Kick the teacher down the stairs.
    Goodbye books, goodbye school,
    Goodbye teacher, you silly old fool.
    No more pencils, no more books,
    No more teacher's dirty looks.

17. Mine eyes have seen the glory of the burning of the school,
    We have tortured every teacher, we have broken every rule,
    We have trampled in the halls
    And written cuss words on the walls,
    While the school was burning down.
    Glory, glory hallelujah,
    Teacher hit me with a ruler,
    I bopped her on the bean with a rotten tangerine
    While the school was burning down.

18. Filea mea, my one-time Latinity
    For many a year has now left my vicinity,
    Sed nihilominous, atque laetitibus,
    Hoc est materia dare militibus
    (But nevertheless and with several whoops,
    That's the stuff to give the troops.)

19. God made the bees,
    The bees make honey,
    We do the work,
    The teacher gets the money.

•••

1. This verse comes from Goose Bay.

2. This anonymous verse appears in *Hamilton Highlights*, a school year-book from Goose Bay, 1966.

3. This parody of Tennyson's "Break, Break, Break" appears anonymously in *Labradorite*, II, from Henry Gordon Academy in Cartwright, Labrador, 1970.

4. According to Jack Fitzgerald, one of the St. Patrick's School girls found a bottle of liquor hidden on Monk's Lane and they decided to raffle it off towards a May 24 camping trip.

7. This parody of the Christmas carol "Joy to the World" is known almost universally now, but this version was given to me by a child in Cartwright, Labrador.

8. B.F.C. is Bishop Feild College.

9. This anonymous verse appears at the beginning of Edith M. Manuel's text *Newfoundland, Our Province*, intended for grades five and six, as revised in 1952. Note that the reference to Aboriginal people is in the past tense, embedding into our school curriculum the notion that there are no longer any people of Indian or Inuit descent in Newfoundland and Labrador. This stands in contrast to *A Canadian Child's ABC*, which patronizingly admits, "They still are here, but their fierce pride / And wild free life have passed away; / Another race has thrust aside / The children of a bygone day."

10. According to *Bartlett's Familiar Quotations*, "Multiplication Is Vexation" comes from an anonymous Elizabethan manuscript of 1570.

11. Attributed to various people. George Story says it came from William Coaker.

13. These alphabet verses were used to teach elocution. I remembered

the first three letters inaccurately, but my sister Janet Kelly was able to get as far as F, which I believe had something to do with "forty fat frogs."

14. Submitted by Peggy Bird to *Lockwood Magazine*, Sandwich Bay, Cartwright, Labrador.

16. Queen Victoria was born on May 24, after which it became the official birthday of the British monarch and the start of the trouting season in Newfoundland.

17. Variations of this parody of "The Battle Hymn of the Republic," sung to the tune of "John Brown's Body," are known in both North America and England. I'm not sure I have this local version exactly right, but it is close.

18. Written by my father, J.M.F. McGrath, to celebrate my sister Elizabeth's passing a Latin exam.

19. From *Folk Speech*, Book 1, by John Widdowson.

John Cabot Was A Holy Man

7. Historic Rhymes

Much is made these days of how mad for history people in New-foundland and Labrador are. In my experience, it was always thus. We were descended from seafarers, so the events of the larger world were also of interest. My grandfather's brothers worked in the shipping business in New York, Great-uncle Arch died of yellow fever while helping to build the Panama Canal, my father served as a ship's surgeon on a voyage to the Canary Islands before he married my mother, and I had innumerable relatives who were serving as religious or medical missionaries in such far-flung places as Peru, Malawi, and China. Of course, we were true little colonials, and everything we knew about these places related to the British Empire, but we could find them on a map, and we knew what their stamps and coins looked like.

Perhaps it was because we were not such ancient citizens as the Beothuk, the Innu, or the Inuit, yet not newcomers like the majority of other North Americans, but as children we had a very strong sense of our place in history. Our schools, homes, and playgrounds were the battle-grounds of the French and English and even the Germans. The Powder-house Mutineers were hanged for treason near my grandmother's potato patch on Belvedere Street, and we once dug up a musket and human bones from our soccer pitch on The Boulevard, so we were all ears when Miss Caroline Furlong told us about the history of "our country."

In grade six we were considered responsible enough to leave the school without a teacher and we used to go to the old Furlong house on Winter Avenue to take our Newfoundland history lessons. Classes were held in the parlour, there would be a small fire in the grate, regardless of the weather, and, if it was fine out, the long windows would be opened onto the lawn. Miss Caroline would stand in the doorway and point with her stick to show us where the Battle of Quidi Vidi had been fought and then we would be sent to Mr. Bob's library to see it on the maps. We weren't allowed to touch the muskets, but we could handle the cannon balls that had been dug out of the garden.

Newfoundland history was a passion for many of us and we almost all counted among our ancestors a good many rebels and rogues, jailbirds and dissenters, ship's captains, and military heroes and heroines. Certain of my classmates were said to be descendants of the pirates Peter Easton and Henry Mainwaring; Miss Rogerson, who had charge of the cloakroom at school, had been an ambulance driver in the war, and my cousin Elsie Doyle had been an army nurse. The little ditties we learned at school were not about history, they were about us, about our people and our lives.

1. You gallants all o' the English blood,
   Why don't you sail the ocean's flood,
   I protest you're not all worth a filbert,
   If once compared to Sir Humphrey Gilbert.

2. Sweet creatures, did you truly understand,
   The pleasant life you'd live in Newfoundland,
   You would with tears desire to be brought thither,
   I wish you, when you go, fair wind, fair weather:
   For if you with the passage can dispense,
   When you are there, I know you'll ne'er come thence.

3. If Poole were a fish pool
   And the men of Poole fish,
   There'd be a pact for the devil
   And fish for his dish.

4. Ye finny monsters of the deep,
   Lift up your heads and shout
   Ye codfish from your hollows creep,
   And wag your tails about.

5. The codfish now in shoals come on the coast
   A Fish'ry this, our Nation's chiefest boast.

6. Cavalier, Cavalier, who's for the king?
   "I," said Sir David, "will help him to bring.
   Here in my colony, safe will he be,
   From Roundheads and Puritans over the sea."
   Cavalier, Cavalier, shall his flag fly?
   "I," said Sir David, "will keep it on high.
   Over my colony shall it float free,
   Forever maintained by my people and me."

7. There lies a land in the west and north,
   Whither the bravest men went forth,
   And daunted not by fog and ice
   They reached at last to a paradise.
   Full two thousand miles it lay
   Washed by a sea of English grey,
   And they named it Newfoundland at sight;
   It's rather the land of Heart's Delight.

8. The fishermen who built me here
   Have long ago hauled in their nets,
   But in this vast cathedral
   Not a solitary stone forgets
   The eager hearts, the willing hands,
   Of those who laboured and were glad,
   Unstintingly to give to God
   Not part, but all of what they had.

9. See how the farmer sows his seed,
   He stands correct to take his heed,
   He stamps his feet and he smacks his hand,
   And turns all round to view the land.

10. John Cabot was a holy man,
    I hope he goes to heaven,
    For he discovered Newfoundland
    In fourteen-ninety-seven.

11. No taxation
    Without representation.

12. A little bit o' Heaven fell from out the sky one day
    And landed on the ocean not so very far away,
    And when the angels found it, sure it looked so sweet and grand
    They elected Joey Smallwood and they called it Newfoundland.

13. J' nos'nallons pour Terr'neuve,
    C'hest nouot pays d'Esden,
    J' vos en dounnai la prevue,
    J'en sis soeux et certain.
    Pour li man coeu soupier!
    Oh man biau p'tit pays,
    Je t'adouor, je t'admire,
    Pus meme que Gerry.

14. "What shall we do for linen?"
    Said the Shan Van Vocht;
    "We'll go to the Inniskillin
    And we'll flay an orange villain,
    And we'll wear his skin for linen,"
    Says the Shan Van Vocht.

• • •

1. According to Karl Samuelson, this verse is Elizabethan, but he gives no source. Sir Humphrey Gilbert took formal possession of Newfoundland as England's first colony in 1583.

2. "Sweet Creatures" was written by Robert Hayman at Harbour Grace in 1628, as an ode to the women settlers of Newfoundland. It was included in his book *Quodlibits*.

3. Recorded in *Seldom* by Dawn Rae Downton.

4. This anonymous verse is from the eighteenth century; recorded in Albert C. Jensen's *The Cod*.

5. From "Labrador: A Poetical Epistle" by George Cartwright, who lived and traded in Labrador from 1770 to 1786.

6. "Cavalier, Cavalier" was written about Sir David Kirke, and appears in the school textbook *More Stories of Newfoundland* by Frances B. Briffett. Kirke lived and worked in the colony of Avalon at Ferryland from 1638 until his death in 1654. He died in an English prison, charged with not paying taxes. His wife continued to run the colony for several more decades until the settlement was plundered by Dutch raiders.

7. "There Lies a Land" was written by P.E. Goldsmith, and quoted in Margaret Duley's *The Caribou Hut*. It is part of a longer poem published in *The Times*, 1917, about the Newfoundland Regiment. The last verse is a repeat of this, the first, with the lines "Full two thousand miles it lay / Washed by a sea of English grey" replaced by "A land to be won by those who durst / No wonder the English chose it first."

8. This anonymous verse about the Basilica of St. John the Baptist was reproduced in a pamphlet about the Presentation Convent and reprinted in *Once upon a Mine* by Wendy Martin from *A Guide to the Basilica of St. John the Baptist*, 1984.

9. "See How the Farmer Sows His Seed" was recorded by Kelly Russell from Rufus Guinchard as a dance rhyme. It comes from the old folksong "Oats and Beans and Barley Grow," a variant of which is in John Widdowson's *Folk Speech*, Book I, identified as a ring game. A section of that song also appears in "Very Well Done, Said Johnny Brown," as recorded by Otto Tucker.

10. "John Cabot" was a mnemonic, similar to "In fourteen hundred and ninety-two / Columbus sailed the ocean blue" or "The Spanish Armada met its fate / In fifteen hundred and eighty-eight."

11. This slogan of the 1828 supporters of Home Rule appears in George Rose's *Cod: The Ecological History*.

12. "A Little Bit of Heaven" is a parody of a sentimental Irish song. In my memory I associate it with Joan Morrissey.

13. This poem, which is written in the patois of the Channel Islands, is probably meant to be ironic. It was composed by a J.S. in 1829, and published by John Sullivan in 1886. The translation reads: "We are going to Newfoundland, / It is our garden of Eden, / Thereof I will give you the proof, / Of which I am sure and certain. / For her my heart sighs! / O my fair little country, / I adore thee, I admire thee, / Even more than Jersey."

14. This rhyme comes from Les Harris's *Growing Up with Verse*. I had heard it previously on a recording, I think by Theresa Doyle, and had come across several other references to it, but didn't take ownership of it until I heard it sung as part of Rick Boland's play "Mutiny" about the Powderhouse Mutineers. There is a monument to the soldiers, who were hanged, on the corner of Barnes Road and Belvedere Street. The Shan Van Vocht, or the Sean-bhean Bhocht, is Irish for the Poor Old Woman, "a personification of Ireland current in the eighteenth-century." The song, which has been called "the Marseillaise of Ireland," dates from the 1798 uprising, when my father's family fled to Newfoundland from Waterford.

Never Eat Shredded Wheat

8. Mnemonics

Much has been written about why mnemonics work, what particular combination of logic and illogic, patterning and fracturing, helps the brain retain certain difficult sequences. Apparently, I know the postal code of the CBC in Toronto (M5W 1E6 or "Make five wieners; I'll eat six"), precisely because it is illogical. One thing I do understand is that rhyme has long been an aid to memory. When something is said or written in verse it is so much easier to memorize and retain. I can remember poems that I learned in grade school, even when I cannot remember my own postal code, never mind the CBC's.

An old Icelandic adage for getting to North America says, "Sail south until the butter melts and then turn right." Those directions are easy to remember, but what about finding your way around the Offer Wadhams? In 1756, a British naval officer named Wadham wrote a song that was placed on record in the Admiralty Court in London shortly after it was composed because it was the best coasting guide to that part of Newfoundland available at the time. More than forty sealing vessels were crushed in the ice at the Offer Wadhams in 1852, and several hundred crewmen escaped because they knew their way around the islands, thanks to Wadham's verse. My father knew the song by heart, and so did a good many others.

Unlike the Vikings, many of our Newfoundland fishermen were illiterate, but that didn't mean they weren't smart. They often composed and memorized navigational aids, and did complicated mathematical calculations in their heads. Women, too, used unusual mnemonics, and a famous recipe for "Old Scripture Cake" begins "1 cup Judges 5:25" (milk), "2 cups Jeremiah 6:20" (sugar), and so on to Solomon's advice in Proverbs 23:4—"beat her with a rod."

I chose two baby rhymes to begin this section on mnemonics, because, until recently, you were never too young to learn about navigation, and I have also included the almost universally known "I Before E" and "Thirty Days Hath September" because I still find them useful. My hope is that someday soon, someone will invent a mnemonic for me to remember all those passwords and PIN numbers I have been told never to write down. I think I prefer the kind of world where "Sail south until the butter melts" is the key to unlocking new worlds.

1. Never
   Eat
   Shredded
   Wheat.

2. Captain on the ocean
   Sailor on the sea,
   The compass comes around to point
   And it points at thee.

3. Keep on the southern side,
   Always on the southern side,
   Keep on the southern side of the point.
   It will help you every day
   When the wind is down the bay,
   If you keep on the southern side of the point.

4. When Hussey's Rock do wet his crown,
   Inside of that you must not be found.

5. When Bill Pott's Point you is abreast,
   Dane's Rock bears due West,
   And West Nor'West you must steer,
   'Til Brimstone head do appear,
   The Tickle's narrow, not very wide,
   The deepest water's on the starboard side,
   When in the harbour you is shot,
   Four fathoms you has got.

6. There's hair on me head,
   There's none on me toes,
   There's woods on Cape Mutton,
   There's none at the poles,
   Back of Trepassey
   Lies all rocks and shoals.

7. When all three lights we see ahead
   We port the helm and show the red;
   Green to green and red to red
   Perfect safety go ahead.
   If to our starboard red appear,
   It is our duty to keep clear,
   To act as judgment says is proper,
   To port or starboard back or stop her.
   But when upon our port is seen,
   A steamer's starboard light of green,
   There's naught for me to do but see
   That green to port keep clear of me.
   Both in safety and in doubt
   We always keep a good lookout;
   In danger with no room to turn,
   We ease her, stop her, go astern.

8. Conception, Trinity, Bonavista Bay,
   Notre Dame, White Bay, Hare Bay, Hi:
   Pistolet Bay at the top of the land—
   Watch out for bears if there you stand!
   Ingornachoix, that lovely bay,
   And down the Strait to the mountains so high,
   Bonne, Bay of Islands, and Port au Port,
   St. Georges, and round by Isle aux Morts—
   La Poile Bay, Heritage, Fortune then roam,
   Placentia, St. Mary's, Trepassey, and home.

9. Labrador we love it so,
   With things to do and places to go;
   Great big land, lots of snow,
   Listen while we tell you places we know:
   Goose Bay, Happy Valley, Port Hope Simpson,
   North West River, Wabush, Labrador City,
   Charlottetown, Hopedale, Churchill Falls,
   Mud Lake, Cartwright, Black Tickle,
   Postville, Rigolet, Makkovik, Nain,
   Battle Harbour, Spotted Island, Forteau,
   Kinnamish, Kinemau,
   Some of our places, we have more,
   All a part of Labrador.

10. I before e, except after c,
    Or when sounded as a,
    As in neighbour and weigh.

11. Thirty days hath September,
    April, June and November,
    All the rest have thirty-one
    Except February which stands alone,
    Which hath but twenty-eight days clear,
    And twenty-nine in each leap year.

12. With seven good mornings, a week has gone by,
    And in fifty-two weeks the year will soon fly,
    One summer, one autumn, one winter, one spring,
    Then you're a year older, and so's everything.

13. Two and two is four,
    And two is a couple of more,
    This one and that one,
    And the two in the road is a knitch.

14. Hoist the peak of your foresail,
    Lower the peak of your mainsail,
    Hoist away on your outside jib,
    And lower your topmast staysail.

15. Twelve were chosen and their names,
    Were Andrew, Peter, John and James,
    Thomas and Bartholomew,
    Matthew and Philip too,
    James the lesser, James the greater,
    Simon the zealot and Judas the traitor.

16. In Genesis the world was made,
    In Exodus the March was told,
    Leviticus contains the law,
    In Numbers are the tribes enrolled.

17. The Ram, the Bull, the Heavenly twins,
    Next the Crab, the Lion shines
    The Virgin and the Scales,
    The Scorpion, Archer, and Sea Goat,
    The Man that holds the watering pot,
    And Fish with glittering tails.

18. From Gready Head steer North by West
    'Til George's Island is come by,
    Then let her go at East-Northeast
    To where the White Bear Islands lie.

• • •

1. "Never Eat Shredded Wheat" is the simplest mnemonic for remembering North, East, South, West—the points of the compass.

2. "Captain on the Ocean" is a children's counting-out rhyme.

3. From Ron Pollett in *The Outport Millionaire*. Pollett was from New Harbour, Trinity Bay. Quoted by Joan Skogan in the *Newfoundland Quarterly* (Winter 2003/4), p. 45.

4. Hussey's Rock is in the area just outside Western Head Tickle in Green Bay. This verse was recorded by Calvin D. Evans in *For Love of a Woman*.

6. From Bern Keating's *The Grand Banks*, and other sources.

7. The simplest mnemonic for sailing is the two lines of "Green to green or red to red, / In perfect safety go ahead." This longer version was recorded by Captain John Froude in his diaries.

8. If I recall correctly, we were expected to be able to draw a freehand map of Newfoundland, labelling all the major bays and towns, by the time we were in grade six. This mnemonic, which appeared in later school texts, was probably an aid to completing the assignment as it takes the student around the island, and "home" to St. John's.

9. Strictly speaking, this isn't a mnemonic so much as an homage. It was composed by the grade three students of North Star School in 1978 and appears in *Songs of Labrador*.

12. The Opies trace the earliest written English version of this verse to 1577, but there are earlier French and Latin ones that go back to at least the thirteenth century.

13. "Two and two" is a mnemonic for counting out ten objects, such as rinds, boughs, or fish. A bundle of ten things is a *knitch*.

14. Les Harris believes that "Hoist the Peak of Your Foresail" is "instructions for some particular maneuver" though he doesn't know what it is.

15. "Twelve Were Chosen," a mnemonic for remembering the apostles, comes from "1882" in *Looking Back: Stories of Fort Amherst*.

16. "In Genesis" lists the first five books of the Old Testament. Recorded by Frances A. Clarke in *Do What You Can*.

17. "The Ram" contains the signs of the zodiac.

18. "From Gready Head" is a fragment from a verse called "The Coastal Pilot," giving the compass courses of the schooner runs. From *For Love of a Woman* by Calvin D. Evans.

The Lord Said Unto Moses

9. Prayers and Take-offs

Religion was a huge part of life in Newfoundland and Labrador during my childhood, even for those who weren't religious. One was as aware of being Catholic or Protestant or Jewish as one was of being a boy or a girl, and, if there was any doubt, any fuzzy edges such as those created by mixed-marriage parents, the resulting social disapproval was just as significant. My family was firmly and unquestionably Roman Catholic, and those of us who were agnostics or atheists were still Roman Catholic agnostics and atheists.

Religion was not a joking matter in our household. There were very few subjects that were off-limits, and religion could be discussed but it had to be discussed seriously. Prayer was not spontaneous, it tended to be private, and it was felt to be more efficacious in Latin. Grace was recited only on formal occasions such as Christmas, or if there was a priest present at the table, but there was still a certain reverence for the act of eating together and there was no greater sin than to waste or spoil food deliberately.

I knew very few of the prayers and parodies I have recorded here, but my friends among the separated brethren could reel them off with no trouble at all. Some are secular, of the *Royal Reader* variety, and others clearly originate with religious institutions. Obviously, not everyone took religion as seriously as my family did.

Even in these more secular times, I found myself a little reluctant to record parodies of prayers and it was a relief to discover that I wasn't the only one who still carried the burden of a religious upbringing. The Protestant friend who gave me the verse which begins "Holy Mary Mother of God, / Send us down a herring scrod" told me that his grandmother tore it out of a friendship book, not because it was irreligious but because it was "too Roman." She was probably right, as a verse such as that one is just the kind of practical, sensible prayer that might have passed muster in our house, if only it had been written in the language of ancient Rome.

1. Matthew, Mark, Luke and John,
   Bless the bed that I lie on,
   Four angels guard my bed,
   Two at the foot and two at the head,
   One to watch and one to pray,
   And two to carry my soul away.

2. O let us ever humbly pray
   That grace to us be given,
   May we be ready to forgive,
   That we may be forgiven.

3. To do unto others as I would
   That they should do to me,
   Will make me honest, kind and good,
   As children ought to be.

4. Thank the Lord,
   Thank the missus,
   Last one done
   Does the dishes.

5. Good, better, best,
   May you never rest,
   'Til your good is better
   And your better best.

6. May God above look down in love
   Upon this leg of mutton,
   Ten days ago 'twas fit to eat,
   But now, by George, 'tis rotten.

7. Jesus sends the weary,
   Calm and sweet repose,
   Helps the tired traveller,
   Blow his runny nose.

8. Many hundred years ago,
   I venture to remark,
   That Noah had some carpenters
   To help him build the ark,
   But sad to say on that last day
   That Noah entered in,
   Those carpenters were left outside
   And punished for their sin.

9. Here's to great King David,
   Who with one stone the great Goliath slew,
   But when he slept with Uriah's wife,
   He found he needed two.

10. Lord bless the food upon these dishes,
    As thou didst bless the loaves and fishes,
    And like the sugar in our tea
    May all our lives be stirred by Thee.

11. Father, Son and Holy Ghost,
    Who eats the fastest gets the most.

12. Rub-a-dub-dub,   13. Past the lips and over the gums,
    Thanks for the grub.   Look out stomach here it comes.

14. Heavenly Father bless us,
    And keep us all alive,
    There's ten of us for dinner
    And not enough for five.

15. Bless me father for I have sinned,
    Fourteen times I broke me wind.

16. Holy Mary Mother of God,
    Send us down a herring scrod,
    When the herring scrod is done,
    Send us down another one.

17. This night when I lay down to sleep,
    I throw my bones in a crooked heap,
    If I should die before I wake,
    Then I will be clear of this toothache.

18. Now I lay me down to sleep
    In my little truckle bed,
    If I should die before I wake,
    How will I know I'm dead?

19. Now I lay me down to snore,
    Insured for fifteen thousand more,
    If I should die before I wake,
    My wife will get her first big break.

20. Matthew, Mark,
    Luke and John,
    You take the wheelbar'
    And I'll dodge along.

21. Attend to your church, the parson cries,
    To church each fair one goes,
    The old go there to close their eyes,
    The young to eye their clothes.

22. Matthew, Mark, Luke and John,
    Hold the horse 'til I get on.

23. Thou shalt not covet thy neighbour's wife,
    His ox thou shalt not slaughter,
    But thank the Lord, it's not a sin
    To covet thy neighbour's daughter.

24. I don't care if it rains or freezes,
    I am safe in the arms of Jesus,
    I am Jesus' little lamb,
    Yes, by Jesus, yes I am.

25. The Lord said unto Moses,
    Luff and weather every squall!
    Moses didn't heed the Lord
    And didn't luff at all.

• • •

1. Recorded by Les Harris in *Growing Up with Verse*. The Opies say this is a prayer "from Popish times," known as the "White Paternoster."

2. *Royal Reader*, Book 1.

3. *Royal Reader*, Book 2.

4. From Ronnie Elson, Happy Valley, Labrador.

5. From *Seldom* by Dawn Rae Downton, and elsewhere.

7. A parody of "Now The Day Is Over" from Elliot Merrick.

8. From *Life's Difficult Moments* by Luke Foote of Lamaline.

9. Recorded by Les Harris in *Growing Up with Verse*.

10. Recorded in *From Caplin Bay 1920 to Calvert 1995*.

14. From *Inter Nos* (1927-34). *Inter Nos* was the annual literary journal of Mercy College, and was edited by my aunt Elizabeth McGrath Conroy [Mennie] for a number of years. I suspect much of the occasional verse was collected or written by her.

15. "Bless Me Father" comes from Patrick Kavanagh of Harbour Main, in his novel *Gaff Topsails*. The events of the book take place at midsummer and it is one of the best books you can read to get a sense of the place folk-lore held in the lives of young Newfoundlanders.

16. From Gordon Williams, recorded originally in his mother's friendship book, which dated back to the turn of the last century.

19. "Now I Lay Me Down to Snore" has been attributed to Eddie Cantor.

20. From Gary Saunders in *Free Wind Home*, a parody of the "White Pater-noster" or night spell. The Opies record a variation from Scotland: "Matthew, Mark, Luke and John, / Hold the horse while I get on. / When I got on I could not ride, / I fell off and I broke my side."

21. Recorded by Tom Quilliam in *Look 'Ere Me Son*.

22. From Gary Saunders's *Free Wind Home*.

25. From Les Harris, who suggests it was something of a game to create odd sayings after the first line. He also gives the example "The Lord said unto Moses / People who smoke short pipes have burnt noses."

Onery, Ewery, Eckery, Ann

10. Language

When I was growing up, my parents spoke French when they didn't want us younger children to know what they were saying. When they did not want even the older children to be privy to the conversation, they were likely to switch to Latin. Most of the time, however, my parents spoke plain, ordinary, Newfoundland English, to which my father sometimes added a smattering of what he called Irish.

I was an adult before I realized how rich that language was and how fortunate I was to have been exposed to it. I knew the difference between a doodleaddle and a drung, a ronker and a rampser, and if my father roared "Out dogs and in dieters," I understood that we kids were to clear out of the kitchen. If Mother said the bread was dunchy, I knew it was heavy but eatable, but, if it was fousty, it was fit only for the ducks.

At school we were given elocution lessons by Lady Outerbridge, but the aim was to have us speak loudly and clearly, not to make us sound like little English girls and boys. At home, we were more likely to be corrected on how to use a word than how to pronounce it, and woe to the child who was caught making fun of "baymen." The majority of our household had been born around the bay, and were proud of the fact. I loved the way the kids from St. Mary's said "ski-ule" instead of "skool" and I wished I had the nerve to imitate them.

Secret or magic languages are part of childhood. Although I never did get a good handle on French, I could speak Pig Latin as quickly as I spoke ordinary English, and I learned to recognize the humour in Dr. Barban's puns, Uncle Alain Frecker's mangled idioms, and the wordplay of the rhymes and jokes told in the schoolyard.

We all knew that the counting-out rhyme "Eeney, Meenie, Miney, Mo" was not English, and I don't think we ever believed that "Onery, Ewery,

Eckery, Ann" was Irish, but it was fun to say these mysteriously attractive words. Folklorists now tell us that "Eeney, Meenie" is an ancient form of Welsh, with over fifty versions known in the United States alone, so perhaps we were really carrying on traditional knowledge without being aware of it.

I have long been convinced that nursery rhymes are a wonderful learning tool for teaching literary analysis. Even the most dunder-headed student knows a few, and can clap out the rhythm, count out the rhyme, and identify the figures of speech. When you add a little humour, acquiring new language skills becomes a good deal of fun, the way it was when we were children, and, before you know it, you're disentangling a Shakespearean sonnet.

> 1. Boyibus kissibus sweet girlorum,
>   Giribus likibus want someorum,
>   Popibus hearibus sweet kissorum,
>   Kikibus boyibus out the doorum.
>   Darkibus nightibus no lightorum
>   Dogibus bitibus pants and torum.

> 2. Onery, ewery, eckery, Ann,
>   Fiosey, folishy, Nicholas John,
>   Qaskery, quarsry, Irish Mary,
>   Sinkalum, stankilum, buck.

> 3. A young theologian named Fiddle,
>   Refused to accept his degree,
>   For, he said, 'tis enough to be Fiddle,
>   Without being Fiddle D.D.

> 4. Oh a man lay down by a sewer,
>   And by the sewer he died,
>   And at the coroner's inquest,
>   They called it sewer side.

> 5. Amo, amant, amas,
>   I love a lass;
>   Amamis, amatis, amat,
>   I knocked her flat.

> 6. Amo, amas, amat,
>   A momma, a tatis, a kint.

7. Eeny, clapsy, whirl around the bapsy,
   Right hand, left hand, high teen, low,
   Touch your heel, touch your toes,
   Cross your legs and under she goes.

8. When twins came, their father, Paddy Dunn,
   Gave "Edward" as a name to each son.
   When folks said "Absurd!"
   He replied "Ain't you heard
   That two Eds are better than one?"

9. Said the shoe to the stocking,
   "I'll put a hole in you."
   Said the stocking to the shoe,
   "I'll be darned if you do."

10. Dip a cup of alusa,
    Sy and dipsey coo,
    Sy and dipsy ky o ramma,
    Gee oh niggy poo.

11. Rose's are red,
    Violet's are white,
    I saw 'em on the clothesline
    Last Monday night.

12. There are many pronunciations
    Of good old Newfound*land*,
    Why there are so many
    It's hard to understand,
    There's *New*finlind
    And New*found*land
    But though it may sound goofy,
    We'd rather pronounce it any way
    Than call the country Newfy!

13. Understand,
    It's Newfound*land*.

14. Dis, dat, dese and dose,
    Dese is all the tings I knows.

15. YY you are
   Y Y U B
   I C U R
   YY for me

16. Hickory dickory dock,
   The mice ran up the clock,
   The clock struck one,
   But the other got away.

17. Up the mountain,
   Slippery as glass,
   Down comes the billy-goat,
   Ridin' on his ... overcoat.

• • •

1. This charming example of phony Latin came from Gordon Williams.

2. "Onery, Ewery, Eckery, Ann" is known as Irish counting. There are similar verses for Chinese and other languages. There are several version of this recorded by P.K. Devine in *In the Good Old Days*, but this version comes from Andy Jones. The Opies trace it back almost 200 years in both England and America.

5. "Amo, Amas, Amat" is emended here to make a cynical comment on love. I collected it from a woman divorce lawyer.

6. The Yiddish of the Latin verb to love becomes "I love, you love, he loves, a mother, a father, a child," as declined by Dr. Albert (Tommy) Wilansky in 1937. This first appeared in his newspaper, *The Familydom*.

7. "Eeny Clapsy" is a nonsense verse for a ball-bouncing game.

8. The failure of certain sectors of our population to pronounce their "aitches" seems to have been a perennial target of self-declared wags. According to the *Dictionary of Newfoundland English*, the most common variation of pronunciation in Newfoundland involves "[h] inserted before initial vowels of stressed syllables (or [h] omitted where educated speakers usually pronounce it)." This verse also makes use of a folk motif of twins called by the same name for comic purposes, such as in the John White ballad "Signal Hill." In reality, if a baby died, the name was often

given to the next baby of that sex born into the family, so that siblings might resort to distinguishing between the two children by referring to them as "Patsy One" and "Patsy Two."

10. "Dip a Cup of Alusa" is a nonsense verse, but an anonymous author claimed it was an Innu lullaby, learned from a grandmother who was bought for a box of cut nails at Little Bay Islands. Several knowledgeable Innu-aimun speakers have looked this verse over and cannot distinguish any Innu-aimun characteristics, so it may be made up or the language has been so distorted that it is impossible to restore any of it to its original condition.

12. This verse, published by Sybil Maclean in the *Atlantic Guardian* in 1947, is an early example of objection to the "N" word, which was said to have been introduced by the American military during the Second World War as a disdainful way to identify locals while visiting "Newfyjohn" or St. John's.

13. It was said that this mnemonic for correct pronunciation was created to teach CBC announcers the proper way to say the name of the new province after Confederation in 1949. It has taken over fifty years, apparently, but eventually it worked.

14. This verse was a favourite way to tease outporters (and some townies) for their pronunciation.

15. "YY" is read as two Ys, or too wise.

16. The ambiguity of English is exploited here. It was interesting to see at what point my grandsons and their friends began to get the humour of knock-knock jokes. Some appreciated the play on words as young as three and four years, while others at five and six still didn't really understand why people were laughing.

17. This is an example of an ambushed shocker—the guilt of saying (or thinking) a rude word is transferred from the reciter to the listener.

They're Good, By Gosh

11. Advertisements and Jingles

"Chug-a-lug a mug of Dominion." "If your clothes aren't becoming to you, you should be coming to us." "Take a tip, try Top Tone." "Fight cancer with a checkup and a cheque." "You can't beat Munns, b'y." I was always fascinated by advertising slogans and jingles, but I came by it honestly because for a time I worked in the business. I wasn't an ad writer, but my sister was and, when I was eight or nine, she shanghaied me and some of my siblings into acting in her spots on some of the early, live television done at CJON.

In the beginning, my brother and I were the Brookfield Ice Cream kids on the Greg Bonner show. We had to eat cold mashed potato in ice cream cones because the lights were so hot that real ice cream would melt all over your hand before the one-minute ads were done. Then I was on "The Early Show" with John Nolan, doing ads for Ayre and Sons. I advertised everything from bunk beds to ladies' hats and Mother's Day presents. Once, George Smith, the set designer, built me a beautiful outdoor ice rink, using a thick mirror, for an ad for figure skates. I practiced my twirls ahead of time without incident, but, on-air, the mirror cracked and I couldn't have looked more frightened if there had been six feet of real water underneath.

I think part of what made the whole advertising business fun was that it was local. Listeners and viewers knew all the announcers like Dennis Ferry, Don Jamieson, Bob Lewis (whose remarkable real name was Clarence Englebrecht), and Mengie Shulman. The window dressers were clever and flamboyant men like Jimmy Long and Paddy Brogan, who also did sets for local amateur theatrics. Vera Smith, George's wife, was the Cream of the West flour woman. Robin Hood had Omar Blondahl singing their ditties, and Myer Frelich sang everyone else's, or that's what we believed.

There were also, of course, parodies of advertisements. The famous Pepsodent toothpaste commercial, which in the U.S. became "You'll wonder where your money went / If so-and-so is president," in Newfoundland became "You'll wonder where your teeth all went / When you brush your teeth with a hockey stick." Many of the parodies were rude, such as the verse that begins "Carnation milk is simply grand, / I always keep a can on hand." Ask anybody over the age of fifty and you will hear the rest.

The debate over the famous legislated exemption for oleomargarine (allowing coloured margarine to be sold) that so inflamed the anti-confederates and so enriched the Crosbie empire when the Terms of Union with Canada were signed, inspired a series of pro-confederate ads (reputedly written by Greg Power). They included: "I pray that I shall never know / A future without Oleo, / Or live to see my little sons / Turn up their noses at my buns."

It's amazing how those early advertisements penetrated our brain pans. I'm sure if you stood in the middle of the Ship Pub today and started singing the Terra Nova Motors song, you'd have everyone up playing imaginary maracas and cha-cha-ing around the room in no time.

1. Smallwood's boots for lads and lasses,
   Smallwood's boots they suit all classes,
   Smallwood's boots they are so grand,
   They are the best in Newfoundland.

2. Drink Dominion, drink divine,
   An ale that far surpasses wine,
   It outshines rum and homebrew fine,
   It's even better than moonshine.

3. Oh this is the place where the fishermen gather,
   With miners, shop keepers, and loggers so hale,
   For sold in this tavern is only the finest,
   And top of the list is Dominion Pale Ale.

4. Rowing in a dory with a Venco in your home,
   You'll be so contented, there'll be no need to roam,
   For the oil you save will pay,
   For the job installed today;
   I wouldn't have a home without a Venco.

5. Keep the home fires burning
   With Venco heat by Learning,
   Save with Venco right away
   And you'll slave no more.

6. If you're looking for a new car, my friend,
   It's Terra Nova Motors we recommend,
   Now is the very best time to buy
   And here is the man who will tell you why.

7. When you buy from us, you can buy wholesale,
   You can get from a caplin to a whale,
   I christened it just Arctic Steak,
   It's the best of meat, it's no fake.

8. From the far, far East to the sunny South,
   We freeze and dry, then ship them out,
   Smoked fish, salt fish, canned or cooked,
   To tell it all we need a book.
   From a caplin to a whale
   Wholesale or retail,
   Phone 726-8890.

9. The whole gang's in favour
   Of that tasty Brookfield flavour.

10. For quality, for zest,   11. Keep bright,
    India is best.   By Snow White.

12. That's a sweet little Alice Blue Gown.
    Did you buy it somewhere in the town?
    So smart and so new, it looks lovely on you,
    Won't you tell where you bought it,
    Please, I'm asking you.

It's no secret, the whole town can see,
From the Premier Garment Company,
It has new style sensation, and what valuation,
That sweet little Alice Blue Gown.

13. Any bottles, big or small,
    Bobby Hudson buys them all.

14. Beer is the very best drink on the course,
    Beer is the drink when from barking you're hoarse,
    It cures indigestion and all inward pains,
    Drop in for a bottle and ask for Sam Haynes.

15. Cocomalt, Cocomalt,
    That's why we all say;
    Every boy and girl should drink
    A glass or more each day.

16. Cocomalt! Cocomalt! That's what we all say,
    Oh, what fun it is to drink a glass or more each day.
    Cocomalt! Cocomalt! We like to drink our fill.
    Mixed with water it tastes grand; with milk it's better still!

17. Cream of the West flour,
    Always the best flour,
    Always the best for your baking.
    Best flour in Newfoundland,
    Made just for Newfoundland,
    That's why whenever you're baking
    Try Cream of the West,
    Always the best,
    Always the best for your baking.

18. Robin Hood makes your pastry so tasty,
    And in your bread Robin Hood puts the good,
    And the cake that you bake will be better for the sake
    Of the touch of "no-sift ever" Robin Hood.

19. For smokers' ease,
    Say Players, please.

20. Seeking perfection?
    Make Gems your selection.

21. Harvey's Hard Bread:
    A cake a day
    Keeps the dentist away.

22. They're good, by gosh,
    'Cause they're made by Koch.

23. If you don't want it read,
    Have it shred!

24. Jack Sprat could eat no fat,
    His wife could eat no lean,
    But with the aid of HP sauce
    They licked their platters clean.

25. I'm a real live wire
    And I never tire,
    It is I who make 'em hot,
    I can cook your meals
    Turn the factory wheels,
    'Cause I'm Reddi Kilowatt.

26. The trend
    Is your friend.

27. You just can't beat
    Electric heat.

28. We worked at Job's fishplant
    As well you all know,
    We worked through the rain
    And the wind and the snow,
    And when the work's over
    We're ready to go.

29. Red, White and Blue means savings for you
    Big travel bargains, all through the year
    Here's all you do to save with Red, White and Blue,
    Pick the rate, go CN.

30. The gray-beard calls for it to wet his throttle,
    On every housewife's table it will be,
    The infant cries to get it in his bottle,
    Even the dog loves Golden Pheasant tea.

31. Hark, the herald angels sing,
    Beecham's pills are just the thing,
    Take them, they are meek and mild,
    Two for a man and one for a child.

32. Oh! This soap is so popular,
    'Tis used in every bay;
    Some call it the White Naptha,
    And I'm sure it's come to stay.
    Now the merchants who stock this soap,
    They say it's selling well,
    And the men who manufacture it,
    Are Proctor and Gamble.

33. Hi, good morning,
    Good Luck the whole year through,
    And if you like a tasty spread,
    Spread it thick upon your bread,
    Sweeter, fresher every day,
    Good Luck, you'll say.

34. You've got a lot to live,
    Pepsi's got a lot to give.

35. We've heard of many brands of shoes,
    And footwear that is fine,
    But Koch shoes is a household word
    That's a favourite down the line.

36. When and where you want to go,
    Call Crotty Taxi, nine-eight-oh.

37. Three blind mice, three thieving rats,
    See how they run, see how they run,
    They all smell a meal of Hobson's Paste,
    And Hobson's Paste is good to taste,
    But it killed all six in greatest haste,
    Three blind mice, three dead rats.

38. You've got oil slicks on your offshore,
    You've got ospreys in your hair,
    And environmental problems
    That would tax a millionaire,
    You're desperate for someone
    Who can sort it out for you,
    Just call John Pratt at Factory Lane
    If you're inclined to sue.

39. See Jack White
    He will treat you right.

• • •

1. The Smallwood boot and shoe company on Water Street was run by David Smallwood, great-uncle to the famous premier, Joseph R. It features fictionally in Wayne Johnston's *The Colony of Unrequited Dreams*. This verse was quoted in Art Rockwood's *Newfoundland and Labrador Trivia: The Sequel.*

2-3. Dominion Ale was put out by the Bennett Brewing Company, which ran a weekly jingle competition in the *Sunday Herald* during the late forties and fifties. The prize was a box of Ganong chocolates for the best submitted jingle.

4-5. The Venco ads were said to have been written by owner Ed Learning, who is thought to have written advertisements for other companies as well. He and Myer (Mickey) Frelich were believed to have written most of the advertising jingles used on radio from the thirties through to the fifties.

6. In the 1950s, Terra Nova Motors sold Pontiac, Buick, and Vauxhall cars, and GMC trucks. The "man who will tell you why" was usually Bob Lewis, an announcer with CJON television and radio.

7. This Arctic steak ad was one of many put out for the Newfoundland Whaling Company; from the *Dictionary of Newfoundland English.*

8. An advertisement for Fort Amherst Sea Foods.

9. The Brookfield Ice Cream company was established in Nova Scotia and was imported to Newfoundland by McMurdo and Co. It later expanded throughout the province. This ad was from 1974, but may have been used for some years by then.

10. This 1959 ad for India Pale Ale was produced by the Newfoundland Brewery. Their logo was a Newfoundland dog called India.

11. Snow White was a laundry on Aldershot Street. This was their ad in 1959.

12. Myer Frelich, a member of the famous Uncle Tim's Barn Dance band, wrote the "Alice Blue Gown" parody for the Premier Garment Company. The Premier Garment slogan was "If your clothes aren't becoming to you, you should be coming to us." This verse was quoted in Art Rockwood's *Newfoundland and Labrador Trivia: The Sequel*.

14. Sam Haynes was advertising his beer tent in the 1913 Regatta Program. Quoted in Jack Fitzgerald's *A Day at the Races*.

15. Cocomalt was advertised as "a nutritionally rich beverage high in calcium and vitamin D." The Commission of Government began distributing Cocomalt free to schoolchildren in Newfoundland and Labrador in 1936. Gary Saunders has speculated that Lady Hope Simpson wrote the Cocomalt jingle, which was printed in a pamphlet extolling the virtues of the supplement and which was sung to the tune of "Jingle Bells."

16. This second, longer version of the Cocomalt jingle is from the Victoria Cove School Magazine.

17. Advertisements claimed that Cream of the West flour was "made just for Newfoundland" because in 1944 the Commission of Government introduced white flour enriched with riboflavin, thiamine, niacin, and iron. The legislated change meant that some popular brands of flour

could not be sold in Newfoundland and Labrador, but it went some way towards solving the dietary problems that were rampant in the country at that time. This verse was quoted in Art Rockwood's *Newfoundland and Labrador Trivia: The Sequel.*

18. The Robin Hood song was written by Omar Blondahl, a radio personality and folk singer.

19. Players cigarettes were made at the tobacco factory behind Rawlins Cross. As a promotional giveaway, they distributed a wooden box-opener, shaped rather like a small cricket bat, that my mother used to threaten to whack my younger brother with. When he knew he'd earned a licking, he'd take off up the stairs howling "Don't hit me with the Players, please," "Players, please!" being the slogan printed on the blade.

20. Gems were cigarettes. Most tobacco products were imported into Newfoundland and Labrador ready-made, but there were two tobacco factories in St. John's, the Newfoundland Tobacco Works and the Victoria Tobacco Works. Both folded before the turn of the nineteenth century, and, in 1902, the Imperial Tobacco Company established a branch on Flavin Street.

21. Harvey's hard bread was hard tack or Hamburg bread, used in the Newfoundland national dish, fish and brewis. The bread would be soaked in water all night, heated through on the stove in the morning, and either mixed with freshened salt fish or served by itself with lashings of molasses. The mill at Rennies River used to pack the bread with a hammer in the top of each barrel to break up the cakes.

22. The Koch shoe factory in Harbour Grace was established in 1953, using government start-up money. In 1957 it got a contract to produce 56,000 pairs of boots for the Canadian Air Force, but it lost the contract twelve years later and went into liquidation. Terra Nova Shoes bought up the assets.

23. "Have it shred" was the slogan of Boland's Security Service in 2002.

24. The HP sauce ad was published in *The Day of Dawn* church magazine.

25. Reddi Kilowatt was the cartoon logo of the Newfoundland Light and Power Company.

26. "The trend / Is your friend" is a radio business slogan.

29. "Red, White and Blue" was sung to the tune of "Hey, Look Me Over."

30. The Golden Pheasant Tea ad was copied from an advertisement painted on the side of a building in downtown St. John's.

31. The Beecham's Pills parody must be one of the best known in the world. Two or three versions of it turn up in Newfoundland and Labrador.

32. "The Song of the P. & G. White Naptha Soap" came from the *Doyle Songbook*.

33. The "Good Luck" song came from Christine Davies at the CBC Archives.

34. This ad for Pepsi was printed in *Newfoundland Stories and Ballads* 17.1 (1970).

35. The ad for Koch Shoes was in *New-Land Magazine* (Autumn 1969).

37. This ad, from *The Old Time Songs and Poetry of Newfoundland*, an earlier version of the *Doyle Songbook*, informed readers that "One tube of Hobson's Rat and Roach Paste killed 106 rats."

38. I wrote this as one of a series of advertisements for lawyers for a Daisy Committee (the historical committee of the Bar Association) event at the L.S.P.U. Hall. The verses were written in imitation of Johnny Burke's "Advertisers Ditty," which included such verses as "Do you want to save

some money and leave something to your wife? / Then call on C. O'N. Conroy in the Confederation Life, / And if you are a poor man and your income it is small, / Just drop into the Law Chambers and they soon will tell you all." "C. O'N." stood for Charles O'Neill Conroy, who later went to work for the Reids out of the Railway Station at Riverhead where the Railway and Coastal Museum now is.

39. An advertisement for City Furniture Co., in the *Newfoundland Quarterly* (1978).

Use It Up, Wear It Out

12. Proverbs and Sampler Sayings

Proverbs have the advantage of being brief, practical, memorable, and, in some cases, witty. Many of the following proverbs and verses could pass muster anywhere in the English-speaking world, but the ones that obviously come from Newfoundland and Labrador give us an interesting take on folk life and traditions. "Let no man steal your lines" says everything there is to say about a fisherman's life, and "There's no knowing the mind of a squid" is equally profound about people.

Although I hate the ubiquitous bar-plaques that you buy in souvenir shops, I find the little framed proverbs that still remain in the houses of relocated communities to be strangely moving. Often cut or copied from newspapers or greeting cards, the very fact that they have survived abandonment suggests that they command a certain respect as avatars of wisdom.

Sampler sayings are generally more thoughtful, as you can copy or cut out a card in minutes but it might take weeks or months to make a sampler. I have two samplers, one from 1892 and one from 1993, but both are alphabets. However, there was a wonderful collection of samplers at the Basilica museum in 2007, done by the nuns who taught us at school.

Ours was not the kind of contemplative household that encouraged embroidery, although my mother was a more-than-capable seamstress and could spin, weave, and do beautiful smocking. The only proverb I can recall being posted in our house was on the fridge: "If you can't wash dishes, don't eat!" I'm not sure how practical that was, but it was certainly memorable.

1. A promise made
   Is a debt unpaid.

2. *Semper ubi sub ubi!*
   Always wear underwear!

3. See a pin and pick it up,
   All the day you'll have good luck.

4. Chop your sticks on Sunday,
   Hump your back on Monday.

5. Yoke your goat and fix your fence,
   A gallon of liver is twenty cents.

6. Use it up,
   Wear it out,
   Make it do
   Or do without.

7. Be a good Methodist,
   Say your prayers,
   And buy your goods
   At Steers and Ayres.

8. If drink is the lift
   On which you depend,
   It's better to pass up
   The event, my friend.

9. The sound of the sea shell in your ear
   Is like a wave when it comes near.
   It is whispering to you its own little secret;
   Whatever it is, be sure and keep it.

10. He who will not, when he may,
    When he will, will have nay.

11. It cannot be bought,
    It cannot be sold,
    Time holds changes
    Which cannot be told.

12. Sewing clothes upon thy back,
    Want and poverty never lack.

13. 'Tis bad enough to lose our health
    But worse a hundredfold
    To give one's self away for wealth
    And sell the soul for gold.

14. Coppers will grow into silver,
    And silver will grow into gold,
    And this you will find very useful,
    To help you, my boy, when you're old.

15. Shear your sheep in May
    And you'll shear your sheep away.

16. Buy a broom in May
    Sweep your family away.

17. Come when you're called,
    Do as you're bidden,
    Go when you're told
    And you won't be chidden.

18. In a leaky punt with a broken oar,
    It's always best to hug the shore.

19. Sew on your back,
    Never have a tack.

20. Old ways,
    Busy days.

21. A whistling woman and crowing hen
    Is good for neither God nor men.

22. Fish and brewis,
    Pork fat and that.

23. Of all the words of tongue and pen,
    The saddest are "It might have been."

24. Never one without two,
    Cold and hunger deeds to rue,
    Never two without a three
    Death and sorrow come to thee.

25. Thieves, whether rich or poor,
    Are miserable and scuddy;
    The fellow who would stoop to steal
    Is laughing at his buddy.

26. There's a pretty little proverb
    From the sunny land of Spain,
    But in North-land as in South-land
    What it means is clear and plain.
    Lock it up within your heart,
    Never lose or lend it—
    "It takes two to make a quarrel,
    One can always end it."

27. The man who brags with dieter's knees
    Is not the first to take the breeze.

28. As you go through life
    Make this your goal:
    Watch the doughnut
    Not the hole.

29. A wit's a feather,
    A tyrant's a rod,
    But an honest man
    Is the noblest work of God.

30. A nodding beam or pig of lead
    May hurt the very ablest head.

31. He who agrees against his will
    Is of the same opinion still.

32. Plant your seed in a row,
    One for pheasant, one for crow,
    One to eat and one to grow.

33. If you want to live and thrive,
    Let a spider run alive.

34. Contentment, parent of delight,
    So much a stranger to our sight,
    Say, goddess, in what happy place
    Mortals behold thy blooming face.

35. 'Twas in the barren isle of Newfoundland
    In Port de Grave this sampler first was plann'd,
    Stitched by a clear unerring marking rule
    At the Newfoundland public Central School
    Where the pure Word of God cannot lie,
    Is read to teach us how to live and die.
    May I with friends and teachers number'd be
    By Grace through Christ in God's great family
    And through eternity that love adore
    Which sav'd from woe a child call'd Fanny Daw.

• • •

1. "A Promise Made" was recorded by Chesley Lethbridge of Cartwright, Labrador, in *A Life of Challenge*.

2. This Latin "motto" came from the boys of St. Bon's.

3. "See a Pin" has an American variant: "See a pin, let it lay, / You'll want that pin another day."

4. "Chop Your Sticks" is a warning not to break the Sabbath. This version comes from Patrick Kavanagh's *Gaff Topsails*.

5. A goat yoke was a triangular wooden collar that kept the goats out of the garden, while liver was cod liver oil, a staple of the economy. If liver

prices were down, it was important to take care of other sources of food. This verse comes from the *Dictionary of Newfoundland English*.

6. Tom Furlong claimed this was a Second World War slogan, but it is so widespread that it probably predated the war.

7. It was the practice for all Newfoundlanders and Labradorians to buy from co-religionists whenever possible.

8. This saying was from an anti-drinking and anti-smoking advertisement, probably aimed at tuberculosis patients.

10. From Joe Blake, Northwest River, 1967.

11. Gwendolyn Watkins, in *Expressions*, the yearbook of Robert Leckie High School, Goose Bay, Labrador.

12. From Mrs. King Ludlow, Change Islands.

13. "'Tis bad enough to lose your health" is a needlepoint interpretation of Ecclesiastes 5, by Sarah Jane Whitmarsh and Anne Winsor from Greenspond, done in 1857.

14. Quoted by Helen Porter in *Below the Bridge*.

15. This common expression was recorded in Tilting.

16. From Les Harris and others.

17. From Les Harris and others.

19. This saying is a variation of number 12.

20. "Old Ways, Busy Days" comes from the Labrador Straits.

21. I first had this saying quoted to me by Peter Levitz, when I was about twelve and had just learned to whistle. I was shocked, as it was my moth-

er, a very fine whistler, who had finally managed to teach me to whistle and I was excessively proud of the accomplishment, as I was a very slow learner. It was recorded in R.F. Sparkes's *The Winds Softly Sigh*.

22. From Pasadena, summing up the Newfoundland diet.

26. From the *Royal Crown Readers*, Book 2.

27. From Nellie Strowbridge's *The Newfoundland Tongue*. She does not explain what this means, but a dieter is essentially a servant who exchanges winter board for his labour, so perhaps the suggestion is that a person who is not being appropriately recompensed will not be the first to tackle a job. Possibly "brags" should read "begs." Where I had multiple versions of some verses, errors such as this often crept in.

28. From *Seldom* by Dawn Rae Downton.

29. Quoted by John Carrick Greene in *Of Fish and Family*.

30. This proverb is borrowed from sailing terminology. A lead pig is ballast or pig iron.

31. Recorded by Ethel Humphries.

32. From *Folk Speech*, Book I, by John Widdowson.

33. It's bad luck to kill a spider. From *Folk Speech*, Book I, by John Widdowson.

34. From a sampler by Rachel Parsons, May 5, 1827, photographed by Antonia McGrath for an article by Anne Chafe in the *Newfoundland Quarterly* (Winter 1985).

35. Stitched by Frances Daw, aged 11, in 1837. The sampler is now at The Rooms and was quoted by Anne Chafe in the *Newfoundland Quarterly* in the Winter 1985 issue.

Tar Mops and Bark Pots

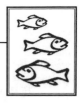

13. The Fishery

I grew up with the scent of salt fish in the air. Even though I lived at the back of the town, when bad weather drove the White Fleet into the harbour, or when the weather was humid, the smell of fish would creep up over the hill, past the Basilica, and then trickle down Bonaventure Avenue to compete with the odour of hops from the Newfoundland Brewery and the cows over in the fields of the Belvedere Orphanage. The smell of money, some called it.

I remember being slightly ashamed when the American kids from Pepperrell complained about the smell, but then I had never lived near the slaughterhouses of Chicago, the smokestacks of New York, or the sulphurous rivers of Maine. I secretly liked the smell of salt fish, and hops, too, for that matter. At school, I had been taught that both harvest and manufacture were admirable occupations and "where there's muck, there's brass."

Even though we were townies, the fishery was all around us. Down on the waterfront, we saw schooners and ships coming in stuffed to the gunnels with salt cod. On the street, men hawked fresh fish, going door to door and assuring skeptics like my mother that "It died in the cart, Ma'am." Out in Horse Cove, we begged the Stapleton men to take us in their boats when they went to check their salmon nets and lobster traps, and when we got back to St. Mary's, we stood by with a bucket to buy cod tongues from the boys while our fathers discussed the season's catch.

Everything always came back to the fishery. Your father might be a brewer, but, when the fishing was poor, the beer didn't sell. If the price of shrimp was low or the herring fishery failed, the bills weren't paid and the doctors and lawyers tightened their belts. Later, my brother built a longliner of his own, and at various times other men in the family worked with him, just as our forebears had when my grandfather was fishing from a jack-boat in Placentia Bay.

For a time, it seemed as if the fishery was no longer relevant to my life, but then I married an admiralty lawyer, and came full circle. Once again, the family finances rested with who was catching what, when, and where. If the fishery was good, the bills were paid, and, if it was poor, then you tightened your belt a bit. It seemed to me only fair that like the scent of cod, the profit trickled up and down, a little more or less to the lawyers and doctors as well as to the fishermen and plant workers.

1. Tar mops and bark pots
   Fishin' caplin to the rocks!

2. Red Rock Ground is the ground for fish;
   Red Rock Ground, no other place,
   Set out your lines and drift around,
   No other place like Red Rock Ground.

3. John Antle got a quintal,
   John Pew got a few,
   John Warr'n got narn,
   And that was all was got this marn.

4. The fisherman's wife, she hasn't much ease,
   She's out on the stagehead in slop to her knees,
   She spends her day weeding with the hot sun o'erhead,
   What splendid fine women our island has bred.

5. The codfish lays a thousand eggs,
   The homely hen lays one,
   The codfish never cackles
   To tell you when she's done,
   And so we scorn the codfish
   While the humble hen we prize,
   Which only goes to show you
   That it pays to advertise.

6. We fished all summer,
   We fished all fall,
   And when it was over
   We'd nothing at all.

7. Rowin' in a dory
   On the Banks of Newfoundland,
   Rowin' in a dory
   With a codfish in my hand,
   I'm happy as a clam,
   Sayin' "How ya gettin' on?"
   Oh what fun a-rowin' in a dory.

8. The first of May
   Is Collar Day,
   When you're called
   You must obey,
   When you're shipped
   You can't run away.

9. For the fish we must prepare
   Our traps and trawls and finger stalls,
   Rubber boots and killick claws,
   Some lines and twines and ropes and coils,
   You get sore hands and full of boils.

10. If your trawler hit a sunker
    And your nets are in a knot,
    And you meant to get a license
    But regrettably forgot,
    If you have a little trouble
    With an excess cod or two,
    Just call John Joy at Factory Lane,
    He'll tell you what to do.

11. Down, down on the deep blue sea,
    Catching fishies for my tea.

12. Fishy wishy come to my hook,
    You be the skipper and I'll be the cook.

13. There once was a man from Kenamu,
    Caught his first fish when he was two,
    It was six feet long, it looked like King Kong,
    And wore one gigantic pink shoe.

14. Holy Moses, what a job,
    Catching connors by the gob.

15. The potheads are coming,
    The whales are in sight,
    The water is foaming
    Out there in the bight,
    Get ready your motorboats,
    Make no delay
    'Cause there's thousands of potheads
    In Trinity Bay.

16. We chased them all day
    'Til we had them in shot,
    And in less than an hour
    We had them in the pot.

17. Lives of great men all remind us,
    We should make our lives sublime,
    And departing leave behind us,
    Something for the hook and line.

18. The codfish lie dead in the ocean,
    The codfish lie dead in the sea;
    They all died of water pollution
    Caused by the oil companies.

19. The caplin is coming
    Right up in the bay
    So plenty manure
    This year so they say,
    With cod's head and sound bones
    To spread on the ground,
    There'll be lots of pataties
    This year to go round.

20. Maud Muller on that summer day,
    Spread the fish instead of hay,
    And she looked up as the sun grew duller
    And thought about the government culler.

21. Once you were out in the briny deep
    Trying away from land to keep;
    Your two glassy eyes can see no more—
    What the hell brought you here on shore?
    If you were stewed with spice and pepper,
    I really think you'd eat much better,
    But now you lie in your own juice
    By God, you're fit for no man's use.

• • •

1. From the *Dictionary of Newfoundland English*.

2. From Ron Pollett, *The Outport Millionaire*.

3. "John Antle" is from the *Dictionary of Newfoundland English*, but other variations turn up elsewhere. For example, Cecil H. Parsons from Leading Tickles, in *On My Way*, records "Old Joe Antle got a quintal, / Johnny Crew [Carew?] got a few, / Bill J'arn, he got narn, / And that was all was caught this marn."

4. An anonymous verse from "Fish and Brewis," a dance tune.

5. "The Codfish Lays a Thousand Eggs" is an anonymous American verse, known all around the world. I found it on an advertising pamphlet for the Newfoundland Emporium on Broadway, Corner Brook.

6. From Victor Butler in *Little Nord Easter*.

7. "Rowin' in a Dory" is a parody of "Roamin' in the Gloamin'." I received this verse from my sister Janet Kelly, and later from Marie Devine.

8. "Collar Day" was when men and women signed onto the fishing crews, or "went into collar, a form of indentured servitude." This verse comes from the *Dictionary of Newfoundland English*.

9. From Lewis C. Little of Bonavista Bay, recorded in *Through My Grandfather's Eyes*.

10. Written by this author, in imitation of "The Advertisers' Ditty," as part of a Daisy Committee event for the Newfoundland and Labrador Bar Association.

13. From grade ten student Kent White, Goose High School, 1995.

14. Sometimes this turns up as "Jumpin' Jesus" rather than "Holy Moses," and "catching sculpins by the gob." This version is from Aubrey Tizzard in *On Sloping Ground*.

15. From Aubrey John Woodman, quoted by Willis P. Martin in *Two Outports*, and also in Ron Pollett's *The Outport Millionaire*.

17. Quoted by Major Peter Cashin in the House of Assembly, arguing the necessity of doing something for the fishery and less for the railway. It is a parody of "The Psalm of Life."

18. "The Codfish Lie Dead" was written on a bathroom wall at the Imperial Tavern, Dundas Street, Toronto, and was the inspiration for CODCO's song "The Wild Cod." Recorded in *The Plays of CODCO*, edited by Helen Peters.

20. The culler decides what the price of the fish is, according to how well it has been split and dried. This verse is from the *Dictionary of Newfoundland English*. The name Muller is an unusual one for Newfoundland, but I went to Memorial with someone of that name in 1966 so it is possible Maud Muller was a real person.

21. Les Harris identifies this as an "ode to a codfish rotting on the beach."

The Devil for Fat

14. Sealing

The day my brother returned home from his first sealing voyage stands out in my memory because my mother gave us kids his clothes to burn in the garden. He was a tall, skinny young man when he went to the Front, but he was a lot skinnier when he returned, and it took days of scrubbing to get the smell of the fat off him. We were all green with envy, though, for to go to the seal hunt was every Newfoundland boy's dream.

As an adult travelling with Inuit in the central Arctic, I learned a lot more about sealing than I ever expected, but it was a very different kind of sealing, not the mass slaughter on pans of moving ice that the seal fishery was off the coast of Newfoundland. I learned to sculp a seal, though not as quickly as those professional swilers, and I learned to eat and enjoy raw seal, but I never learned to like the rank stink of old seal fat.

Once, while I was out with some Inuit hunters in the Queen Maud Gulf, they shot a seal and pulled it up onto a pan of ice, but, when they went to sculp it, the animal twitched and writhed, even though it had no head left. I understood then how the animal rights activists managed to get film footage of men apparently skinning live seals. It took ages for that seal to stop moving, and we were all so spooked by it that we sank the carcass and skin and moved on.

As someone who has raised and eaten my own chickens, I have no problem with a humane seal hunt, but I still intended this section on the seal fishery to contain both the pros and cons of the sealing issue. However, the only anti-sealing verse I came across was "Don't buy / While seals die," a slogan of the Humane Society of the United States. I couldn't bring myself to include it as an example of Newfoundland and Labrador rhyme, as it is both silly and uninteresting.

Given the wit and humour of the Codpeace movement, it's no wonder the animal rights crowd has failed to win the propaganda war in New-foundland and Labrador. How can you compare "Don't buy / While seals die" with "In cod we trust"? As a carnivore, I know I'd rather eat seals that lived free and died fast than chow down on battery chickens pumped full of antibiotics and steroids. So this section does not contain both sides of the sealing story—it contains only one side.

1. Old Billy Kay is the devil for fat,
   He can always smell where the swiles is at.
   Old Billy Kay got a fine old bark,
   He strikes the patch before it's dark.

2. Breathes there a man with head so dense,
   Who never said I have better sense
   To improve on nature I should never try
   To spray the white coats with green dye.

3. The furry little creature
   With its coat of snowy white,
   To the sealers—hard earned money
   As the elements they fight.
   Where's our MPs, our government?
   Why don't they intervene,
   To prevent our white coats
   From a-wearin' of the green?

4. Now Terry is a fine young man,
   But he has a lot of jaw,
   He thought he'd do the devil-an-all
   When he got the *Esquimaw*,
   But the *Mary J'yce*
   Was caught in the ice,
   And so was the *Osprey* too,
   And Big Bill Ryan left Terry behind
   To paddle his own canoe.

5. When the ice comes in the bay,
   The seals will soon be here to stay.
   When the ice be packed in tight,
   We kill the seals with all our might.

6. Before you leave the sealer's side,
   The ice or slob must first be tried.

7. The hardy sons of Newfoundland
   Wait not for sealing laws,
   Mid ice and snow they dare to go
   To try and grease their paws.

8. Oh, Greenspond is a pretty place,
   And so is Pinchard's Island,
   Me ma will get a new silk dress
   When Pa comes home from swilin'.

9. Onward Christian sealers,
   Sailing for the Front,
   Don't let those protestors
   Interrupt the hunt.

10. Don't take a girl from up in town,
    They dresses up so fine,
    Take a girl from long the shore
    Can cut your sealskin line,
    Don't take a girl from up the bay,
    Don't take them by their looks,
    Take a girl from down the bay
    Can make your sealskin boots.

11. Oh when I left my native home,
    The tears they fall and blind me,
    When I think on my charming dear,
    The girl I left behind me.
    I am going out to the ice,
    All the crew will join me,
    I'll make a bill and send it to
    The girl I left behind me.

12. Give thanks for our Newfoundland island,
    The land that was given by God,
    Where the natives eat nothing but seal meat,
    And the seals will eat nothing but cod.

• • •

2. Parody of "Breathes there the man with soul so dead, / Who never to himself has said / This is my own, my native land," from "The Last Minstrel" by Sir Walter Scott, from the *Weekend Magazine*, May 13, 1978, p. 8. Anti-sealing protesters spray-painted baby seals green, to spoil their pelts.

3. Recorded by Cynthia Lamson in *Bloody Decks and a Bumper Crop*. The title of the book is an old sealers' toast that I often heard when I was a child.

4. Terry Halloran of the *Esquimaw* was a famous sealing skipper from St. Mary's Bay. I learned this verse from my father.

6. From Jack Fitzgerald, *Untold Stories of Newfoundland*.

7. From Fred Adams's *St. John's: The Last 100 Years*.

8. Great Big Sea sings this verse as "Ma will buy me a new frock coat / When Pa comes home from swilin.'"

9. This is a parody of "Onward Christian Soldiers."

10. From Hiram White of Gillard's Bight.

11. A dance tune I was given by Christina Smith. Variations on this seventeenth-century tune were favoured by the military because it was easy to play on the fife, and it was played whenever a regiment left town or a man-of-war set sail. The tune is also known as "Waxie's Dargle," "The Rambling Labourer," "The Spailpin Fanach," and "Brighton Camp."

12. "Give Thanks" is a take on John Collins Bossidy's "And this is good old Boston, / The home of the bean and the cod." It was the Codpeace Ode, part of the 1970s protest against Greenpeace.

Come on You Slackers

15. War and the Military

For most North American children in the 1950s, 'war' meant the Second World War, but for many Newfoundland children, it evoked a more complicated montage. Our school on Gower Street gave us a good view of both the harbour and Signal Hill, where the ghosts of sailors and soldiers thronged. War loomed large in our young lives, and war was not just cannon balls and muskets from Mr. Bob Furlong's study; it was mustard gas, machine guns, and The Bomb. We knew all about the French invasions of our city, but we also knew about the 710 casualties at Beaumont Hamel. We wore poppies in November and forget-me-nots in July, and Tommy Ricketts, Earl Haig, and the First Five Hundred were as real to us as our grandfathers, and, in some cases, *were* our grandfathers.

We recited "Flanders Fields" from memory in class, and with Miss Hawkins we sang, "The minstrel boy to the war is gone, / In the ranks of death you will find him," knowing that our ancestors hadn't betrayed the motherland, nor would we. When the air-raid sirens went off at noon at Churchill Square, James Lane, and elsewhere, we were all well aware of the implications. War probably did more to shape our sense of who we were—Fighting Newfoundlanders, down to the last boy and girl—than any other single factor in our lives.

War didn't just mean history, though, for we had the American military on our doorstep. There were several American families in our neighbourhood, and we were great friends with one family in particular. I don't know what surprised me more about them—the fact that they were Catholics, or that they ate fish heads like real Newfoundlanders. Captain Fonke had fought in Korea, and there was nothing he liked better than a large cod head boiled up with rice.

Not everyone was as fond of the Americans as we were, though, and when our American cousins and friends began getting drafted to go to Vietnam, we joined the protestors and marched to the American consulate on Kingsbridge Road. By then we were teenagers, and the slogans and verses we chanted were ones we learned from television. But embedded in the backs of our minds were rhymes and chants that were a reflection of our own jumble of contradictory attitudes, some learned on the street and some in the school room.

1. Come on you slackers,
   Now here is your chance
   To show your devotion:
   You're wanted in France.

2. When I am dead and quite forgotten,
   On my tombstone carve this line:
   Esau Penny, First Newfoundlander,
   Mortally wounded by a number nine.

3. In the precincts of this room,
   Cussing you must ban,
   For every cuss-word you let fall,
   A penny in this can.

4. I drink to life and I drink to death,
   I slap my lips with a song,
   For when I die, another I
   Will pass the cup along.

5. Never in a bar or barber's
   Talk of ships or crews or harbours.
   Idle words—things heard or seen—
   Help the lurking submarine.

6. Loose lips
   Sink ships.

7. Roll me over and I'll tell you more,
   Roll me back as I was before.

8. In times of war, but not before
   God and the sailor, we adore;
   The danger past, and ills requited,
   God's forgotten and the sailor slighted.

9. Friends and foes, to battle they goes,
   What they fights about nobody knows.

10. At the siege of Belle Isle,
    I was there all the while,
    All the while, all the while,
    At the siege of Belle Isle.

11. We sailed wherever ship could sail,
    We founded many a mighty state;
    Pray God our greatness may not fail
    Through craven fears of being great.

12. Ram me well and point me fair,
    And I'll drive a ball from here to Cape Spear.

13. First it rained and then it snew,
    Then it friz and then it thew,
    And then it friz again.

14. The Yankees thought they won the war,
    Parlez-vous!
    The Yankees thought they won the war,
    Parlez-vous!
    The Yankees thought they won the war,
    The Newfies won it the day before,
    Inky dinky parlez-vous!
    The Yankees had to scrub the floor,

Parlez-vous!
The Yankees had to scrub the floor,
Parlez-vous!
The Yankees had to scrub the floor,
The Newfies marched right out the door,
Inky dinky parlez-vous!

15. Here's to the American eagle,
    Who never gives a damn,
    But flies over every country
    And shits on Newfoundland.
    Here's to good old Newfoundland,
    So noble and so rich,
    We want no turd from your bastard bird
    So get rid of the son of a bitch.

16. May heaven bless you, Joan Blondell,
    Your form and acting are both swell;
    Let those who curse you go to Joe Batt's Arm
    And there, I bet, they'll do no harm.
    Come back and with us long do dwell,
    For we all love you, Joan Blondell.

17. Courage, brother, do not stumble,
    Though the path be dark as night,
    There's a star to guide the humble,
    Trust in God and do the right.

18. Captain Wilson says we're dirty,
    Armstrong's views are just the same,
    But we never are down-hearted—
    What is dirt compared to shame?

19. Newfoundland is a fine old place
    Can never be forgotten,
    Not by us, the sailors three
    Who stayed with Mrs. Cotton.

• • •

1. From *Memoirs of a Blue Puttee* by Jean Edwards Stacey.

2. Esau Penny was a regimental cook at Gallipoli. The song was to the tune of "My Darling Clementine." Quoted by Jean Edwards Stacey in *Memoirs of a Blue Puttee.*

3. This verse came from the 166th Newfoundland Field Regiment. A "swear box" or "cuss can" was common in bars frequented by the military. There was always one on the bar at the Tudor Inn and at the Crow's Nest.

4. "I Drink to Life" is a toast that also comes from the 166th Newfoundland Field Regiment, recorded by their padre, Rev. W. Charles Hodgins. The toast was originally proposed by British air ace Major Mannock.

5-6. A notice posted around St. John's in 1942 read, "Careless talk costs lives and ships." These verses, which said much the same thing, were well known during the war.

7. Said to be engraved on two sides of a rock that guarded a treasure at Fleur de Lys, and recorded by folklorist Elizabeth Greenleaf in the early 1930s.

8. Captain Joseph Primm quoted this in relation to the Merchant Navy in the *Telegram*, 2006.

9. An old sailor's rhyme.

10. Belle Isle, on the west coast of France, was a British objective in the Seven Years War. The siege lasted for three months in 1761, and, according to the Opies, this verse was used as an endless story to tease children. It seems to have been borrowed into the Newfoundland tradition, because of the similarity of place names, and possibly because of Sir Alexander Schomberg's siege of the Strait of Belle Isle for Wolfe in 1761.

11. "We sailed wherever we could sail" was on the wall of James Dicker's room in Rigolet—it is the motto of the British Overseas Club.

12. "Ram Me Well" is said to have been engraved on a cannon at Maddox Cove.

13. "First It Rained" is a verse from Gander about the Atlantic Air Ferry, a reflection on Newfoundland's infinitely dreadful weather.

15. Recorded by Joan Pike at a wedding in St. Philip's. Les Harris records a shorter version of the same 'toast' and ties it to "the squabbles with Americans over bait and fishing rights on the Newfoundland coast."

16. Joan Blondell was criticized for singing a song about the Newfie Bullet while entertaining the troops, and George Ayre is said to have written this verse in reply.

17. "Courage, Brother" is from a monument in Port Blandford to Charles A. Mesher of Grand Village (now Mud Lake), Labrador, who was killed at Monchy in 1917. It was recorded in *Them Days* magazine.

18. "Captain Wilson Says We're Dirty" was composed by Lt. Colonel A.L. Hadlow, to the tune of "What a Friend We Have in Jesus," in a dugout at Suvla in the First World War.

19. Written in Mabel Cotton's wartime autograph guest book, signed by J. Gardner, Liverpool; A.F. Benjamin, Morden, Surrey; and C.G. Goff, Guilford, Surrey, all of the HMS *Daliah* K59.

Doctor Bell Fell Down the Well

16. Health

I grew up believing that my grandmother was the only survivor of nine siblings, eight of whom died in a cholera epidemic. When my cousin Anna finally tracked down the actual death dates, it was clear our eight little great-aunts and great-uncles died young and heartbreakingly close together, but they were not all victims of the same tragic event. However, that story of the eight dead children brought home to us the fragile nature of life. A child or parent could be alive and healthy one moment and dying the next. Only the intervention of prayer or the doctor could change the outcome.

My father was the sole doctor in a family of lawyers. He told me once that he thought he'd made a pretty good doctor, but, if he had it to do again, he might simply have become a businessman. I think, however, that he liked the privileges being a doctor gave him. Long after he had made administration, nutrition, and public health his life's work, my father was still consulted by his old patients. He was always called sir, never got a parking ticket, and when we came chugging up Prescott Street on our way to the fish shop or the butcher's, the policeman would always stop the other cars to wave us through.

The fifties were not healthy times in Newfoundland, although they were probably better than the thirties and forties. Tuberculosis was still rampant, children still got rickets, gastroenteritis was common, and pneumonia and measles were serious illnesses. Polio was still killing and disfiguring children, and childbirth was something a woman went into with a certain fear and trepidation. Under such conditions, doctors were not little gods, but they were treated like them just in case.

The opposite side of the coin, of course, was evident in the song "Hard Times": "Next comes the doctor, the worst of them all, / Saying what's been the matter with you all the fall. / He says he can cure you of all of your disease, / When your money's all gone you can die if you please." In pre-medicare days, you avoided alienating the doctor and prayed for good health. Today we can thank our secular saint, Tommy Douglas, that, if the doctors can't cure us, at least we aren't left broke and "hauled on the hill."

1. When you cough or sneeze or sniff,
   Be quick, my lad, with your handkerchief.

2. The best six doctors anywhere,
   And no one can deny it,
   Are sunshine, water, air,
   Rest, exercise and diet.

3. Sneeze on Monday,
   Sneeze for danger;
   Sneeze on Tuesday,
   Kiss a stranger;
   Sneeze on Wednesday,
   Get a letter;
   Sneeze on Thursday,
   Something better;
   Sneeze on Friday,
   Sneeze for sorrow;
   Sneeze on Saturday,
   Joy tomorrow.

4. Dr. Bell fell down the well
   And broke his collar bone,
   Doctors should attend the sick
   And leave the well alone.

5. Here I stand upon the scales,
   A plump and rounded figure,
   And if the boys don't like me now
   They sure won't like me bigger.

6. A son of medicine, grave as can be,
   Laughed in his sleeve while pocketing his fee,
   By learned jargon proved his skill so good,
   And talked right well because not understood.

7. Should Lancet Bill an equal taste unfold
   For feeling pulses and for feeling gold,
   Although stark radical, he'd swallow down
   The bitter pill of office from the Crown
   Could pay be got, or dignity or honour,
   All M.D. as he is, he'd push for coroner.
   (Care should be had in sounding this M.D.
   Learning's sworn title, else might seem empty.)

8. Here come the doctors, dear boys,
   No virtue do they lack,
   They're the best of men we ever knew,
   With their courage strong and their faith so true,
   So give three cheers and a tiger, too,
   Because they have come back.

9. You can rattle his bones
   Over the stones,
   He's only a pauper
   That nobody owns.

10. In the woods she cut her finger,
    Stopped it up with turpentine,
    Tore the leg from off her bloomers,
    Tied it up with cotton twine.

11. Went in the woods and cut me finger,
    Bound it up with turpentine,
    Tore the waistband off me trousers,
    Tied it up with fishing line.

12. May the wealthy and great
    Roll in splendour and state,
    I envy them not, I declare it.
    I eat my own ham,
    My own sheep, my own lamb,
    I shear my own fleece and I wear it.
    I have lands, I have bowers,
    I have fruit, I have flowers,
    The lark is my morning alarmer,
    So fare thee well now,
    God speed the plow,
    Long life and success to the farmer.

13. I have no use for scissors or comb
    And I have no place for a louse to roam,
    My head is my own and I don't care,
    I'm so good as you with a head of hair.

14. Christ was of a virgin born
And he was pricked with a thorn,
It did neither bell nor swell
And I trust in Jesus this never will.

• • •

1. "When You Cough" comes from one of the *Royal Readers*.

2. From Clarissa Squires of Seldom, recorded by her daughter Cheryl.

3. From Sandra Cooze's *Roses in December*.

4. Variant of a quatrain in Harry Graham's 1898 *Ruthless Rhymes for Heartless Homes*: "Dr. Jones fell in the well / And died without a moan."

5. "Here I Stand upon the Scales," a parody of a traditional recitation, refers to the weight gain caused by Rimifon, a drug used in the early 1950s for treating TB.

6-7. The verses about the "son of medicine" who laughed up his sleeve, also called Lancet Bill, were written about William Carson, the Great Reformer. The obscure little joke at the end of number 7 plays on the similarity of sound between M.D. and M.T. or empty. Both verses were reported by J.R. Smallwood, from the *Times*, October 1833.

8. The Grenfell doctors, who got three cheers and a tiger, were being greeted by the schoolchildren of St. Anthony when they returned from their summer holidays. The verse was recorded by Phoebe Rich for *Them Days* magazine.

9. "You Can Rattle His Bones" is a rhyme about the former Poor House on Sudbury Street in St. John's, recorded by Fred Adams in *Potpourri of Old St. John's*.

10-11. Of these two verses, the "bloomers" version is the better known. They both refer to the widespread practice of using not commercial turpentine but what is more commonly called myrrh, frankum, or snotty var—the soft resin of fir or spruce—to stop up cuts. There are even claims that a severed finger or toe can be reconnected when bound up with a liberal application of resin bladders wrapped in a bit of rag.

12. "May the Wealthy and Great" came from an old Irish jug owned by the Ledwells of Calvert. It isn't really about medicine but it sounds so very like my father's prescription for good health that I decided it belongs in this section.

13. This is a verse recited by a witch who was bald due to a genetic condition, quoted in Barbara Rieti's *Making Witches*.

14. A variation of this charm to prevent a splinter from festering is in John Widdowson's *Folk Speech*, Book I.

The Railway Is All the Go

17. Travel

Newfoundland men have long been known as travellers, while their wives and daughters stayed home. Such was not the case in my family. Most travel in Newfoundland and Labrador was by boat, of course, but there were other means of getting around and, in her lifetime, my mother tried them all.

It was a point of pride with her that she was the first woman to have a driver's license in Newfoundland. Back in her twenties, when she was an insurance agent for London Life, she had a motorcar of her own and entered—and won—a car race around Quidi Vidi. Race officials tried to stop her from collecting the prize, a small table clock, but she insisted that there was nothing in the rules to say a woman could not compete, and she cherished that clock for the rest of her life, long after rheumatoid arthritis prevented her from driving, or even walking more than a few steps. She loved cars.

My father was the opposite. For him a car, like a horse, was a necessary evil, useful only for getting you from point A to point B, and subject to puzzling and infuriating breakdown. He drove so badly that he was never in an accident because other drivers could see him coming a mile off and would avoid him. He had the bad habit of keeping an open book, face-down on the dash, to wile away the tiresome seconds it took for a red light to change to green, and I once found him in his car, reading at a stop sign, waiting for the light to change while other cars pulled out around him.

My parents began their married life travelling by shank's mare. They walked on their honeymoon from St. John's to Burin, following the railway track through the woods because there were few roads at that time. After my brother Seumas was born in St. John's in December of 1933, my mother flew him home to St. Mary's with Captain Frazer navigating by following the bonfires my father's patients had lit along the way. During the war, my mother took up skiing again and my mother-in-law recalls her skiing with my father from Harbour Grace to Carbonear to inoculate the children at the school. In the 1960s, crippled but still game for adventure, my mother still managed to visit Labrador, where she tried a skidoo for the first time.

It is true that it was mostly men who did the travelling in Newfoundland and Labrador, but women were not entirely stay-at-homes. I have met quite a few in my time who went to the Labrador coastal fishery as cooks when they were as young as eleven years of age. Quite a few northern women ran their own dog teams, including some of the Grenfell nurses, and the distances covered by women like Elizabeth Goudie were prodigious.

The handful of verses here are a reflection of those various modes of travel other than by water: skidoo, dogteam, automobile, horse, train, and even shank's mare.

1. Snap, crack goes my whip,
   I whistle and I sing,
   I jumps upon my double sled
   So happy as a king,
   My horse is always ready,
   And I am never sad,
   There's no one here so happy as
   The double sledder lad.

2. In the olden days of Labrador
   The men used a komatik,
   But now there's a new invention
   Which is safer and it's quick.
   This new machine is yellow,
   It has a motor too,
   This gas-operated dogteam
   Is the Bombardier skidoo.

3. Daddy bought a little car,
   He fed it gasoline;
   And everywhere that Daddy went,
   He walked—our son's eighteen.

4. Famous last words
   About headlights that shine—
   "Well, if he won't dim his,
   Then I won't dim mine."

5. I saw horses wearing snowshoes
   And the dogs that hauled the mail
   From the little town of Deer Lake
   All along the Viking Trail,
   And those hearty guides who led them
   Through the drifts and over the bogs
   Couldn't tell who worked the hardest,
   Those brave mailmen or the dogs.

6. Frank Cleary drives a motor car,
   Foley drives a train,
   Frank Foran drives a horse and gig
   But he gets there just the same.

7. Billy and Tom went in over the pond,
   Two little dogs to haul them along,
   When they got in, the weather come thick,
   And out they come with one little stick.

8. I'll go the way my father went
   As long as I have breath,
   The tracks he left behind him
   Are in the marshes yet.

9. The railway is all the go,
   To Topsail we will flow.
   There on her pebbly strand,
   With our sweethearts hand in hand,
   We will dance to Bennett's Band—
   Lardy dah, lardy dah!

10. As I roved out one fine morning in May
    To view all the labours all on the railway,
    The birds they did whistle and the sun it did shine,
    And I went for amusement on the Riverhead line.

• • •

1. From Rufus Guinchard, recorded by Kelly Russell.

2. From *Hamilton Highlights*, a 1967 Goose Bay school yearbook.

3. From *Legacy of Laughter* by Jack Fitzgerald.

4. From Gordon Williams.

5. "I Saw Horses Wearing Snowshoes" was written by Ned Payne of the Rocky Harbour Pioneer Club.

6. This may be a personalizing variant on the verse, "The fox he's got a bushy tail, / The lion's got a mane, / The rabbit's got no tail at all / But he gets there just the same."

8. This verse was a response to the new road to Point Lance, recorded in *Our Cultural Heritage: A Short History of the Cape Shore Area*.

9. From the *Terra Nova Advocate*, May 4, 1881. Quoted by Aiden O'Hara in the *Newfoundland Quarterly* (Fall 1978), p. 8.

10. Quoted by Aiden O'Hara in the *Newfoundland Quarterly* (Fall 1978), p. 6.

Sally Chaytor Had a Pig

18. Animal Rhymes

There was a time when animals were a part of everyday life in Newfoundland and Labrador. My older siblings, who were brought up round the bay, had daily contact with a cow that provided milk to the family, a horse that my father used to make his rounds, and a series of frequently short-lived dogs, many of whom went "down the Labrador" in spring and, surprisingly, never came back. My own childhood in town boasted more exotic zoology: a snake, a horned toad, various goldfish and turtles, budgies, ducks, numerous dogs, and a hutch full of rabbits that included one particularly cannibalistic and vicious doe that we named after my grandfather's second wife.

Out in the wider world, there was Granfer Stapleton's horse, which I thought was why my parents always called St. Thomas 'Horse Cove.' That horse looked like she was too lazy to chew but she had a speedy and brutal kick and I have the scars to prove it. Down in St. Mary's, where we frequently visited, there was Billy the Ram, of which I was justifiably terrified, and lots and lots of sheep that wandered the road in straggling herds, triangular yokes round their necks to keep them out of the gardens. My mother used to spin and weave wool when she lived down there, although I couldn't imagine her fastidious hands washing and handling the matted and dirty fleece that covered their rumps.

Animals were often the subject of jokes, both against and about them, and sheep were the subject of the first joke I distinctly recall not understanding. "Such-and-such a community had an economic development study and found two new uses for sheep," I overheard a man explain. "Mutton and wool!" Much laughter at the expense of the community named. Sheep were thought to be stupid and filthy, an indication of a backward society. Today, they're an endangered species on the island. As one wag scribbled on the bottom of a government poster urging us to eat local lamb: "Two thousand roving dogs can't be wrong."

My own introduction to domestic animals came in the form of a small flock of hens that I brought from Pouch Cove, who were soon joined by two brave little bantam roosters from Tilting. For a number of years, these lovely birds kept us well supplied with eggs and entertainment, and they even became the subject of a series of poems. It was as the provider for these coopies that I became aware of how prevalent hens once were in both the town and country, and how very many rhymes there were about them.

Many of the animal rhymes I discovered fit into other categories in this collection, but there were so many, not just about hens, but about pigs and horses, dogs and cats, and insects, that they seemed to deserve a bestiary of their own.

1. Fiddle-dee-dee
   Fiddle-dee-dee,
   A horse's head's
   Where his tail should be.

2. Sally Chaytor had a pig,
   And he was double-jointed,
   But when she tried to dance with him,
   She was disappointed.

3. I had a little dog,
   His name was Tiny Tim,
   I put him in the bathtub
   To teach him how to swim.
   First he drank the water,
   Then he ate the soap;
   He died last night
   With a bubble in his throat.

4. I had a dog,
   His name was Rover,
   And when he died
   He died all over.

5. Snail, snail, come out of your shell,
   Or I'll beat you black and blue,
   Your mother and father have gone to hell
   And that's where you'll go too.

6. Snail, snail,
   Come out of your hole,
   Your mother and father
   Are burned in the coal.

7. Snail, snail, draw me a boat,
   For if you don't I'll set you afloat.

8. Beaverthorn
   Put out your horns
   The cows are in your garden.

9. Cock-a-doodle-doo,
   Nanny lost her shoe,
   Grandy lost his walking stick
   And didn't know what to do.

10. Here's the Lord Mayor,
    And here's his two men,
    Here is the rooster,
    And here is the hen,
    Here are the chickens and here they run in,
    Chin chopper, chin chopper
    Chinny chin chin.

11. If I had a donkey
    And he wouldn't go,
    Do you think I'd spank him?
    No, no, no.
    Put him in the stable,
    Keep him nice and warm,
    Best little donkey
    Ever was born.

12. May chicks
    Bring all dicks.

13. Rickety, rickety rocking horse,
    Over the fields we go,
    Rickety, rickety rocking horse,
    Giddyap, giddyap—whoa!

14. I've got a dog as thin as a rail,
    He's got fleas all over his tail,
    Every time his tail goes flop,
    The fleas on the bottom all hop, hop, hop.

15. When a hen lays eggs, with each,
    She is inclined to make a speech.
    The self-same urge stirs human bones
    Whenever men lay cornerstones.

16. I hope that I would never meet
    An animal I'd have to eat,
    Because it would be very cruel
    To slay and eat a little mule.

17. Grasshopper, grasshopper,
    Grasshopper grey,
    Give me some lassie
    To put in my tay.

18. Paul said unto Peter,
    Let's skin a cat and eat her.
    Peter said unto Paul
    Let's eat her skin and all.

19. The placid cow all red and white,
    I love with all my heart,
    She gives me healthful milk to drink,
    And cream for apple tart.

20. Horny, horny billy buck
    How many horns do you hold up?
    Five you say—six you'll get,
    Horny, horny billy buck.

21. When poor old father tried to kill
    The cock-a-doodle-doo,
    They all shouted "Coward,
    He's not as big as you."

22. Pitchy, pitchy butterfly,
    If you don't your mother will cry.

23. Scardey cat,
    To kill a rat.

24. A robin and a wren
    Are God Almighty's cock and hen.

25. Oh the billy goat chased the nanny goat
    Over the hill and tore her petticoat,
    Oh the billy goat chased the nanny goat,
    Over the hills and far away.

26. A crow flew over the river
    With a lump of raw liver.

27. One white foot—try him,
    Two white feet—buy him,
    Three white feet—look well about him,
    Four white feet—go without him.

28. In I come,
    Down I squat,
    Laid an egg
    And up I got.

29. Scratch, scratch, scrabble, scratch,
    Pussy's in the cabbage patch,
    Quick, quick, grab a stick,
    Give that pesky cat a flick!

30. A bear slept in his bear skin,
    He found it nice and cozy,
    But I slept in my bare skin,
    And I nearly frozee.

31. One, two, three,
    Mother caught a flea,
    Flea died, mother cried,
    One, two, three.

32. Catch the bug carefully
    Lay him on the block,
    Then take the mallet
    And give the lad a knock.

33. His horse is called Mountie
    A name we like well,
    And when they're together
    They really look swell.

34. I wish I were a pussy
    With a tail like fluff,
    I'd sit upon your dresser
    And be your powder puff.

35. The little white pullet has laid her first egg,
    It looked like a pipkin, it felt like a keg.
    It wasn't too bad, she said to the hen,
    But I don't think I'm going to do it again.

36. The cow kicked Nelly
    In the belly in the barn;
    Didn't do her any good,
    Didn't do her any harm.

• • •

1. According to the Opies, "The Wonderful Horse, with His Head Where His Tail Ought to Be" was a sideshow attraction at fairs, and those who were tricked into paying to see it went out of their way to trick their friends into paying also. The horse turns up as a riddle or enigma also: "There was a sight near Charing-Cross, / A creature almost like a horse; / But when I came this Beast to see, / The Head was where the Tail should be." The answer is that it was a mare with her tail tied to the manger. The fiddle-dee-dee version I use here came from Ray Guy, who produced it when he heard I was planning to publish a book of nursery rhymes, because "We've got it hinder part before, haven't we? It should have been

nursery rhymes first, and then our own dictionary, encyclopedia, atlas, history and literature. For aren't these ditties for tots the first small steps along the way of Ulysses and the lads, Greek or Irish or Harbour Gracian."

2. A rude version of this verse begins "Sally Chaytor had a cow, / Went to milk her, didn't know how."

3. I got this verse from Donna Morrissey, when we were doing a literacy panel at the Fluvarium in St. John's.

4. From my sister Janet Kelly.

5. From my aunt, Helena McGrath Frecker, in her unpublished manuscript "A Childhood in Avalon."

7. Tom Dawe in *Landwash Days* claimed that the snail would draw pictures with his slime if you said this verse to him. Otto Tucker's version is "Snail, snail, blow out your horn, / Or else I'll kill you, sure as you're born."

8. From the *Dictionary of Newfoundland English*. A beaverthorn is a slug.

10. "Here's the Lord Mayor" is a rhyme for identifying or washing parts of the face: forehead, eyes, nose, mouth, teeth, chin.

11. This verse from Ross Rowsell came from St. Anthony, possibly introduced by one of the Grenfell nurses. According to the Opies, the first two lines are a traditional verse that in 1822 was reworked by Jacob Beuler into a six-verse song mocking the Prevention of Cruelty to Animals Act, sung to the tune of "The White Cockade."

12. "May chicks" (i.e., eggs hatched very early in the season) will be "all dicks," all roosters rather than hens, a proverb that this author found holds true.

13. "Rickety Rocking Horse" is a knee-bouncing rhyme, from Mary Fearon in the *Telegram*, 2005.

14. A hopscotch rhyme from Jack Fitzgerald's *Legacy of Laughter*.

15. From Jack Fitzgerald's *Legacy of Laughter*.

16. From Peter Parsons, a grade seven student, in *Expressions*, Robert Leckie High School yearbook, Goose Bay.

17. Grasshoppers extruded a brown molasses-like liquid when you caught and held them. This version comes from Gary Saunders in *Free Wind Home*, as well as others.

18. From Les Harris, *Growing Up with Verse*.

19. From Gordon Williams.

20. From a woman named Bridgette, from Burin. After the second line, the child said how many spanks he or she would get, and the reciter added one on and, at the end, administered the smacks.

25. "The Billy Goat Chased the Nanny Goat" is a dance rhyme for "The Banks of Newfoundland," also called "Up the Pond." David Benson has suggested it was also a reference to boys and girls from the Southside of St. John's Harbour.

27. Variations on this verse are well known in America, where it is a guide to how to buy a horse.

29. From Mary Bridson, writing in the *Newfoundland Quarterly*.

30. Quoted in "The Recitation" by Lucy McFarlane.

32. From Mose Ingram, who claimed it came with a "con" cure for bedbugs.

35. Some time ago, I took a course in poetry writing from Mary Dalton. I found it impossible to write anything until I followed her advice to begin with what you know best. Nursery rhymes, including this one,

were succeeded by poetic catechisms, and eventually a variety of other poetic genres, until I had the requisite fourteen poems about chickens I needed to complete the course.

36. From Ray Guy. Les Harris records a variation that is a little more sexually explicit: "Oh the ram pucked Nellie / In the bottom of the valley, / Oh the ram pucked Nellie, / Coming home from the barn, / Oh the ram pucked Nellie / In the bottom of the belly, / Did you ever see the funny place / The ram pucked his horn?"

Cows Love Cabbage

19. Love Ditties

I recently watched as my five-year-old grandson laboriously worked preparing valentines for his kindergarten class. Close at hand he had a sheet of instructions, which outlined what types of valentines were acceptable, the necessity for each valentine to be signed and legible, and the list of names of all the children in his class. Unless there was a card for each and every child, none of his valentines would be distributed. It all seemed a bit soulless.

In my own childhood, valentines were anonymous, signed "Guess Who?" or "A Secret Admirer," and you gave valentines to whomever you liked. Nasty ones were discouraged, but you might give common punch-out cards to most friends and construct a few really fancy ones for the boys or girls you had a crush on. It was, in some ways, a popularity contest to see who got the most and the fanciest cards, and while I know I never got the most, I'm pretty sure I didn't get the fewest either.

I can't recall that I was traumatized by my failure to achieve equality with popular playmates like Danny Williams, but I do recall occasionally getting a particularly nice card and being thrilled to think someone out there had special feelings for me.

Our house in town was on a busy street, and there were far too many people hovering around on the doorstep in the evenings to have accommodated "snatchers," but I do remember that these were occasionally a part of the rather sweet and innocent ritual of childhood love. A snatcher was a card attached to a thin string, left on a doorstep, and then "snatched" away just as the recipient reached for it.

Times have changed, and we now have the conviction that if a young person is deprived of his quota of Hallmark cards, he's likely to turn into a high school sniper or something. Steal a kiss in the book closet today and you'll be charged with sexual assault. It should make me nostalgic for the innocent old days, but all it does is make me feel like a grouchy old fogey.

1. There's a rose in the garden for you, young man.
   Pick a pretty girl with the green dress on.

2. The rose is red, the violet is blue,
   Sugar's sweet and so are you.
   If you know who 'tis sent you this,
   When we meet, we'll have a kiss.

3. I wish you luck,
   I wish you joy,
   May the first to fill your cradle,
   Be a curly-headed boy.

4. Mary Mellow,
   Dressed in yellow,
   Out in the hen house
   Kissing her fellow.

5. Speed the sail
   O'er the sea,
   Bring the man
   To marry me.

6. Rosy red apple,
   Gingerbread and tart,
   Tell me the name
   Of your sweetheart.

7. Oat seed I set,
   Oat seed I sow,
   Whoever is my sweetheart
   Come after me and mow.

8. Love is like a head of cabbage
   When it's cut in two;
   The leaves I give to others
   But the heart I give to you.

9. I love coffee, I love tea,
   I love the boys and the boys love me.
   If I go home with a broken knee,
   What will my mother say to me?
   I'll tell my mother to hold her tongue;
   She had a fella when she was young.
   I'll tell my father just the same;
   He had a girl and changed her name.

10. One and one makes two, 'tis true,
    But if these two should marry,
    One and one would then make two,
    And there'd be one to carry.

11. Where there's whispers, there's lies,
    Where there's lassy there's flies,
    Where there's girls, there'll be b'ys.

12. All hail New Moon, all hail to thee,
    New Moon, New Moon, come tell to me,
    The one who my true love shall be.

13. Cows love cabbage,
    Pigs love squash,
    Boys love girls,
    They do, by gosh.

• • •

1. From St. Mary's Bay, probably from Sheila Lee.

3. From George Poole, recorded in *A Lifetime Listening to the Waves*.

5. From Burin, recorded in the *Harbour Grace Standard*, 1883.

7. According to Otto Tucker, "Oat Seed I Set" was the rhyme recited by children on June 21, Hemp Seed Night. Girls gathered timothy hay seeds in small paper bags, and would then dress in their best. Boys would disguise themselves with a brin bag with holes for eyes or blacken their faces with smut for mustaches or eyebrows. When the girls threw the hemp seeds, the boys would chase them and were allowed to kiss the one they caught. This courting game began when children were about ten years old and ceased when they were about fifteen, old enough to be courted for real. A Dorset version, probably the original, can be found in Thomas Hardy's *The Woodlanders*. This version comes from Hilda Chaulk Murray in *More than Fifty Percent*.

8. From Musgrave Harbour, in "Folklore, the School and the Child," a Memorial University M.A. thesis by Sheila Maud Saunders, 1982.

9. From Otto Tucker, who recorded it from his sister, the late Mrs. Flossie Tucker Rowsell.

11. From Suzanna King, Wabush.

12. "All Hail New Moon" was a part of the rituals associated with predicting who you would marry. On Midsummer's Eve some girls would put an egg white in a glass of water, perched on a fence post. The rising sun would cause the egg to form a corpse or a coffin, a bride or a ship. When it was finished, they'd throw the egg in the road and the first person to walk over it would indicate the family who would have someone marry or die. A beautiful description of this can be found in Patrick Kavanagh's novel *Gaff Topsails*. This version of the rhyme came from R.F. Sparkes, *The Winds Softly Sigh*.

13. From St. Mary's Bay, probably from Sheila Lee.

Sad I Are

20. Love Lost

It came as a surprise to me, when compiling all the verses I found related to love, courtship, and marriage, just how cynical so many of them were. There seemed to be far more satiric and even bitter verses than sentimental, sweet ones. I expect this is because folk verses are often the vehicles for socially unacceptable attitudes. The cloying sentiment of the *Royal Readers* and Hallmark cards didn't fare well in the back alleys of St. John's or the fishing rooms of the Labrador coast, but racism, bigotry, and sectarian and scatological verses are common in the folk canon that flourished in such places. Sexism, coming from both genders, also reared its ugly head.

The stock image of the outport wife standing behind her husband at meals, serving him before the children and then serving the children before herself, is one that many older people are familiar with. However, there were reasons for many of these apparently patriarchal tyrannies. Men and women were not treated equally, but the inequity was more complex than simply "He for God and she for God in him."

My husband occasionally makes reference to what he calls "the tyranny of the serving spoon," recalling how his mother would take advantage of having everyone at the table, waiting for the first bite of food, to exercise her power. Whatever she had in her craw had to be expunged before anyone got fed, and that included his father. In my own household, my father acknowledged my mother's decidedly modern, feminist views by insisting she be served second, the baby being the first for the sake of peace and quiet.

The family home might have been owned on paper by the man of the house, but he held no sway there—his domain was the fish store, the loft, or, in town, the garage or potting shed. This separation mirrored the divisions of labour in catching and making fish, a separation that often extended itself into the marriage, that was for hundreds of years insoluble except by an act of the British Parliament.

Not all marriages were created equal. Some were excellent and some were execrable, but all of them at various times suffered from the tension of two separate souls trying to subsume their wishes and desires for the good of the family. Inevitably those tensions would bubble to the surface, and sometimes emerge in verse.

1. I slept and dreamed that life was beauty,
   I woke and found that life was duty.

2. A man works 'til setting sun
   But a woman's work is never done.

3. Men dying, make their will, but wives
   Escape a work so sad.
   Why should they make what all their lives
   The gentle dames have had?

4. Down by the sea shore,
   Carved in stone,
   Four words of caution:
   "Leave the boys alone."

5. Pins and needles,
   Needles and pins,
   When a man marries
   His trouble begins.

6. Look at me now and the day you wed me,
   When you fell in love with all me charms,
   Naked and hungry you have left me,
   Hit me now with the child in me arms.

7. Here's to this good old world of ours,
   Where men are hard to please,
   But women, bless their little hearts,
   Wants everything they sees.

8. A loaf of bread,
   A jug of wine;
   I don't need no
   Valentine.

9. When your husband at you flings
   Forks and knives and other things,
   Seek relief and seek it soon
   With the handle of a broom.

10. A boy is like a bird
    That flies from tree to tree,
    But when he sees another bird
    He thinks no more of thee.

11. Women have a thousand faults,
    While men they have but two:
    Everything they say
    And everything they do.

12. Do you love me or do you not?
    You told me once but I just forgot.

13. Here's to the train that runs on wheels
    That never runs into danger.
    Here's to the girl who sticks to her love
    And never flirts with a stranger.

14. Sad I are,
    Sad I be,
    Knew our love
    Could never was.

15. The crazy girl that gets a kiss,
    Goes home and tells her mother,
    She got to get her lips cut off,
    And never kiss another.

16. Roses are wilted,
    Violets are dead,
    Sugar is lumpy
    And so is your head.

17. My bonny lies over the ocean
    My bonny lies over the seas,
    And when she's not working the Tickle,
    She's back of the Green on her knees.

18. Oh I went up in a dory,
    And I came down in a flat,
    I'm a decent married woman,
    Take your hand outta that.

19. I had an hourglass figure
    When I was in my prime.
    Since then there's been a shifting
    In the sands of time.

20. I for Johnny Cross
    You for stony bladder,
    Keep your wife at home,
    Or else I will get at her.

21. Thread the needle through the bush,
    Thread the needle dandy,
    Thread the needle through the bush
    But don't you come too handy.

22. Many a ship was lost at sea
    For want of sail and rudder,
    Many a boy has lost his girl
    By flirting with another.

23. Margie Moore behind the door,
    Kissed the boys and made 'em roar,
    Her mother came out and gave her a clout
    And turned poor Margie inside out.

24. Marry in white—chosen the right.
    Marry in blue—will always be true.
    Marry in pink—spirits will sink.
    Marry in green—ashamed to be seen.
    Marry in yellow—ashamed of your fellow.

25. Monday for health,
    Tuesday for wealth,
    Wednesday's best of all,
    Thursday for losses,
    Friday for crosses,
    And Saturday's no day at all.

26. Hallowe'en,
    He'd later confess,
    Wasn't the only time
    He wore a dress.

27. When first I seen her
    The leaves was greener,
    The small birds twittered
    From tree to tree.
    I was not delirious
    But cold and serious;
    Now what is the difference
    Between you and me?

• • •

4. From Valerie Whelan, La Scie.

6. "Look at Me Now" is a verse from a James Murphy ballad about an abused wife. When Brian Dunfield made the first of his three unsuccessful attempts to gain office in 1913, supporters of his opponent in the predominantly Protestant district put about the rumour that he was actually Brian O'Dunphy, a Papist. He was trounced. He ran again in St. John's, and this time his election poster featured a photograph of him holding his young son. Some wag scrawled "Hit me now with the child in me arms" across the bottom of it, and before long it was on every poster in town. He lost again.

7. From Mrs. Johnson, recorded in *Stories from Shirley's Haven* by Sheila Lee.

9. Recorded from Kathleen of Tilting by Lucy McFarlane for *Downhome* magazine.

10. Recorded from Gwendolyn by Lucy McFarlane for *Downhome* magazine.

12. Recorded by Lucy McFarlane for *Downhome* magazine.

13. Recorded from S.B., Witless Bay, by Lucy McFarlane for *Downhome* magazine.

14. From Albert Hammond of Portugal Cove, recorded by his daughter Linda Rose.

15. A dance rhyme from Plate Cove recorded by Kelly Russell in *Close to the Floor*.

16. Recorded by Ella Allen, a grade seven student, in *Expressions*, the yearbook of Robert Leckie High School, Goose Bay.

17. "My Bonny Lies over the Ocean" refers to a Bell Island girl who was spreading her favours for cash. I heard it performed by Richard Hanlon at a kitchen party in Portugal Cove, where he brought the house down when he sang "The Little Red Light" in the manner of a nine-year-old girl.

18. From Otto Kelland in *Dories and Dorymen*.

20. "I for Johnny Cross" is said to be the song of the fairies at Johnny Argan's bridge, St. Jacques-Coombs Cove. I have some notion it is from a book by Mike McCarthy.

22. George Riche, in Tim Borlase's *Labrador Songs*, gives this verse as beginning "Many a ship has gone to sea / For want of tar and rudder." I wasn't able to make sense of it until I found the version given here, signed by Don Shipworth, Lincolnshire, October 21, 1941, written in Mabel Cotton's wartime autograph guest book.

23. Given to me by my sister Janet Kelly.

24. "Marry in White" is a prediction game based on the colour of the wedding dress. This version was recorded by Sarah Holwell of Spotted Island for *Them Days* magazine. It also appears in Hilda Chaulk Murray's *More than Fifty Percent*.

25. "Monday for Health" suggests the day of the week on which you should marry. This version was recorded by Hilda Chaulk Murray in *More than Fifty Percent*.

26. By Bill Brodie in the *Globe and Mail*, October 21, 2006.

27. This fragment is from a story titled "Johnny" by my aunt Elizabeth McGrath Conroy [Mennie], printed in *Inter Nos* in 1925, and reprinted in *Catholic World*. She identifies it as a traditional come-all-ye, but I have never found it anywhere else.

Said She Couldn't Dance

21. Dance Tune Rhymes

When I was thirteen years old, I lived at McAuley Hall, a hostel in St. John's for girls from the outports attending Holy Heart of Mary high school. Only the grade eleven girls were allowed to watch television (their viewing was restricted to the news) so the rest of us had to make our own amusements in the evening. Generally, we danced. In the common room, there was a record player and a few scratchy recordings—I remember "Blueberry Hill" and other popular songs—but, fortunately, there was also a girl with an accordion.

I don't remember the accordion player's name—she was older than me and not much of a talker—but she could heave and squeeze that big red box for an hour straight without a break. I soon learned the basic steps for what we called The Lancers, and I still remember clinging for dear life when the bigger girls swung round so fast that I was lifted off my feet. If it was a warm night and we worked up a sweat, your grip would slip and you could be bounced off the wall at high speed.

Like most "fiddlers," our musician couldn't read music and had no notes, yet she never seemed to run out of dance tunes. The only one I recognized was "Mussels in the Corner" which I knew as "Dirty Old Torbay Men," and it was years before I realized that many of the Newfoundland and Labrador dance tunes had words. According to Christina Smith, "Lots of tunes have a little rhyme that goes with them. It helps the fiddler remember how the tune goes, and helps the dancers to keep in time."

The dance rhymes are occasionally sung as the last verse or chorus of the tune, but more of them have passed into the oral tradition as nursery rhymes. Because they are mnemonics, personal to the musician who is using them to recall how the tune goes, you will sometimes find more than one set of words for each tune. Sung or recited, they are often a little bit rude, so they are more likely to be shared privately than publicly.

1. John come sell your fiddle,
   And buy your wife a gown,
   John won't sell his fiddle
   For all the wives in town,
   John won't sell his fiddle
   For fear they'll all go mad,
   Many's the rattling time
   That John and the maidens had.

2. Our old cow, she had her calf,
   Outside the parlour winder,
   Only for the bull we'd have
   No other for the winter.

3. Mudder wouldn't beat him, beat him, beat him,
   Mudder wouldn't beat her only son,
   Mudder wouldn't beat him, beat him, beat him,
   'Cause he was her only one.
   Mudder wouldn't beat him, beat him, beat him,
   Mudder wouldn't beat him, not for fun,
   Mudder wouldn't beat him, beat him, beat him,
   'Cause he was her only son.

4. Some like girls who are pretty in the face,
   Some like girls who are neat around the waist,
   I like a girl with a wiggle and a twist,
   In the bottom of her belly is the cuckoo's nest.

5. The leg of a chicken is very good pickin',
   The leg of a duck, the leg of a duck,
   We'll give it to Nelly to put in her belly,
   The leg of a duck, the leg of a duck.

6. I lost my love and I care not,
   She may come back and she may not,
   But if she do, she's welcome to
   The little bit that I've got.

7. Did you ever go into an Irishman's shanty
     Where water was scarce and whiskey was plenty?
     A stick in the door instead of a latch,
     A three-legged stool, a table, a match.

8. Saturday night I lost my wife,
     And where do you think I found her?
     Up in the moon, humming a tune,
     And forty-five devils around her.

9. There's beef in the cupboard
     And pork on the shelf,
     If no-one don't eat it
     I'll eat it myself.

10. Chase me Charlie,
      I got barley
      Up the leg of me drawers.
      If you don't believe it,
      Come and see it
      Up the leg of me drawers.

11. Sally Ann, she needs a man,
      Her petticoat wants a border,
      Sally Ann, she needs a man,
      Now she's up in the corner.

12. See the women in the boats,
      Rubber hats and rubber coats,
      See the women in the boats,
      Off to Petty Harbour.

13. All the women on Cape Pine
      Sleep in bed 'til half past nine,
      Light their fires with kero-sine,
      Mussels in the corner.

14. Bobby the bull and I fell out.
      What do you think it's all about?
      Up with my boot and give him a clout
      And always sit in the corner.

15. Auntie Mary had a canary
    Up the leg of her drawers,
    While she was sleeping
    I was peeping,
    Up the leg of her drawers.

16. Coming home from the races,
    Bleeding noses and cut faces
    And all as drunk as blazes,
    Coming home from the pond.

17. Cover me up, cover me up,
    Cover me up in the blankets
    And cover me nose over with clothes
    And cover me up in the blankets.

18. Molly wants a beatin', beatin', beatin',
    Molly wants a beatin' down and some,
    Molly wants a beatin', beatin', beatin',
    Molly wants a beatin' on the bum.

19. God bless the first husband I had,
    If he were livin' he wouldn't be dead,
    For many a scunner we had in the bed
    Before daylight in the morning.

20. Tidy Hi she got a new dress,
    Tidy Hi a fine one,
    Tidy Hi she got a new dress
    Made from her mother's old one.

21. She can dance to the flute
    She can dance to the whistle
    She's as neat around the waist
    As a cow around the middle.

22. Molly Mulgrady-o,
    She ate three buckets of praties-o,
    It took three pound to relish 'em down,
    Besides the tail of a leggy-o.

23. Pussy got up in the plum tree,
    Pussy got up in the plum tree
    I'll bet a pound she won't come down
    Until she do get hungry.

24. Young man you kissed my daughter,
    You did, young man, you did, young man,
    You went to the well for water,
    You did, young man, you did, young man.

25. Out all night in the foggy dew
    Tipped her up and kissed her too,
    If you get there before I do,
    Mussels in the corner.

26. I took her on my knee,
    And I began to diddle her,
    Don't you tell my wife,
    Or I will tell the fiddler.

27. Billy Fitton, Billy Fitton, have you seen John White?
    Billy Fitton, Billy Fitton, have you seen John White?
    Billy Fitton, Billy Fitton, have you seen John White?
    Gone around the harbour for to stay all night.
    Gone around the harbour for to get a dozen beer,
    Gone around the harbour and he won't be coming here,
    Gone around the harbour for to get a cuppa tea,
    If you sees the little bugger tell him I wants he.

28. Oh, I wish I had a few more bricks
    To build my chimney higher,
    The cat got up on my old roof
    And pissed down in the fire.

29. I took Sally to a ball,
    Sally couldn't dance at all,
    Stuck her up against a wall,
    Sally is a corker!

30. Did you ever see the devil
    In the garden digging praties,
    And the praties were so small,
    That he couldn't dig them all?

31. Said she couldn't dance,
    Because she had her bloomers on,
    But when she took 'em off
    She could dance as good as anyone.

32. 'Deed I am in love with you,
    Out all night in the foggy dew,
    'Deed I am in love with you
    Mussels in the corner.

33. Sally Brown come down I wants you,
    Heigh ho, roll and go,
    Roll and go, and she rolls me over,
    And I'll spend my money on Sally Brown.

34. Joey Clements I don't care,
    Little ball behind his ear,
    Foxiest man I ever seen
    Foxy Joey Clements.

35. Oh dear mother, what a pain I got,
    Put me on that Charlie pot.

36. Leaves be red,
    Nuts be brown,
    Petticoats up
    And trousers down.

37. Down with the skirts,
    Up with the pants,
    Out on the floor,
    Everybody dance.

38. McTavish is dead and his brother don't know it;
    His brother is dead and McTavish don't know it.
    They're both of them dead and they're in the same bed
    And neither one knows that the other is dead.

39. O'Brien he died of peritonitis,
   His brother he died of chronic arthritis,
   There's both of them died and oh how we cried,
   'Cause neither one knew that the other had died.

40. Aunt Virtue Kean made up this song,
   Out with the doctor all night long.

• • •

1. According to the Opies, Robbie Burns collected a variation on "John come sell your fiddle," which can be traced back to 1694: "O Willie come sell your fiddle / O, sell your fiddle so fine; / O Willie come sell your fiddle / And buy a pint of wine. / If I should sell my fiddle / The world would think I was mad / For mony a rantin day / My fiddle and I hae had." This version came from Moses Harris of Lethbridge, recorded by Kelly Russell in *Close to the Floor: Newfoundland Dance Music.* Russell's *Close to the Floor* and *The Fiddle Music of Newfoundland and Labrador* give the musical notations for many of the dance rhymes in this section.

2. From Christina Smith. Musical notations for many of the dance rhymes found in this section can be found in *The Easiest Dance Tunes from Newfoundland and Labrador* by Christina Smith. Check out www.inshorefiddling.com for more information on Christina's fiddling and teaching methods.

3. From Christina Smith.

4-5. From Kelly Russell, *Close to the Floor.*

8. I heard this on CBC radio on Regatta Day, 2004, to the tune of "Up the Pond."

10. "Chase Me Charlie" comes from Kelly Russell in *Close to the Floor.* The same tune is used for rhymes including "Auntie Mary Had a Canary" and "Paddy Bought a Pig."

11. From Helen Porter in *Below the Bridge.*

12. From Les Harris, *Growing Up with Verse*. My grandson Misha, who is a great fan of Great Big Sea, brought it to my attention that they sing "Here they come as wild as goats, / Children in their little boats, / Women in their petticoats, / Down from Petty Harbour."

13. From Les Harris, *Growing Up with Verse*.

14. From Everett Russell, collected by Evelyn Osborne. Lyrics for this and other dance rhymes can be found in Evelyn Osborne's M.A. thesis, "'We Never Had a Bed Like That for a Violin! We Had a Bag!': Exploring Fiddlers and Dance Music in Newfoundland: Red Cliff, Bonavista Bay and Bay de Verde, Conception Bay," Carleton University, Ottawa, 2003.

15. Recorded by A Crowd of Bold Sharemen.

16. From Jack Fitzgerald's *A Day at the Races*.

17-18. From Gerald Quinton, collected by Evelyn Osborne.

19. From Everett Russell, collected by Evelyn Osborne.

20. From Raymond ("Grampa") Guy of Doting Cove, in *Memory is a Fickle Jade*. Philip Hiscock has speculated that this is a responsive verse to "I's the B'y Who Builds the Boat."

21. From Anne Broderick, collected by Evelyn Osborne.

22. From Gerald Quinton, collected by Evelyn Osborne.

23. Les Harris records this as: "Hi diddle um dee, / Pussy cat up in the plum tree. / Half-a-crown to fetch her down, / Hi diddle um dee."

24. From Gerald Quinton, collected by Evelyn Osborne.

28. From Christina Smith.

29. From Sylvia Quinton Ficken, collected by Evelyn Osborne.

35. This is an incomplete dance rhyme, collected by Christina Smith in Goose Bay.

38-39. The rhymes concerning "McTavish" and "O'Brien" are two verses of the same song with a variation in names, sung to the tune of "The Irish Washerwoman." "McTavish" came from satirist Ray Guy and "O'Brien" from musician Frank Maher.

40. The two-line lyric about "Aunt Virtue Kean" was a response to a woman merchant's song, "Lukey's Boat," which she wrote to mock a man who wouldn't pay his bills. The reply, intended to cast doubt upon Mrs. Kean's virtue (or her hypochondria, some say), only succeeded in crediting her with a song that is known and loved all over Newfoundland.

Be Never Wholly Idle

22. Royal Readers

I once asked an elderly man how far he had gone in school, and he promptly answered that he had gone as far as "The monkeys and the red caps." I recognized at once a reference to a story about a sailor who falls asleep under a tree and has his kitbag rifled by monkeys. This story came from the *Royal Readers*.

By the time I was in school, the *Royal Readers* were long gone from the curriculum, but not from the classroom and not from my teacher's head. On good days, when the work went well, we were rewarded with readings of all the old favourites: "Lucy Gray," "Bruce and the Spider," "Inchcape Rock," Dickens's Little Nell, and snippets or floods of Browning, Sir Walter Scott, Coleridge, and Shakespeare. John Gilpin was one of my favourites, also Dick Turpin, and, although I doubt it really came from those ennobling *Royal Readers*, "The Wreck of the Nancy Belle" with "the cook and the captain bold, / And the mate of the Nancy brig, / And the bosun tight and the midship might / And the crew of the captain's gig."

I was fortunate in that our teacher preferred long, narrative poems about ships and highwaymen. Some of the other *Royal Reader* material could be a bit pious, or dryly factual, like "Sponges grow in the deep, deep sea, / Cork is the bark of a very large tree." She also preferred to hear herself read or recite these works to having our faulty memories butcher them. Not so for many of the older people I came in contact with, particularly in my visits round the bay. They cherished the inspirational old verses they had been made to memorize, and passed them on to me and other children, who to this day can recite them by heart.

According to Dr. A.C. Hunter, writing in the pages of the *Newfoundland Quarterly*, the *Royal Readers* first saw the light in 1870, yet were in print and selling steadily a hundred years later "to parents here in

Newfoundland whose children are not learning to read." I do not know that all the inspirational verses I have collected over the years are *Royal Reader* verses, but they could be. If a verse rhymes and scans, if it teaches some fact or provides a moral or model for behaviour, if it sticks in the head like an advertising jingle but has no crude or crass element, it is probably a remnant of the beloved *Royal Readers* or a fair imitation of the kind of verses those books taught us to respect.

1. Little children, love each other—
   Never give another pain.
   If your brother speak in anger,
   Answer not in wrath again.

2. Love not talk,
   Love not boast;
   Grief comes to him
   Who brags the most.

3. Once I saw a little bird come hop, hop, hop;
   So I cried "Little bird, will you stop, stop, stop?"
   And was going to the window to say "How do you do?"
   But he shook his little tail and away he flew.

4. I would not in a cage be shut
   Though it of gold should be;
   I love best in the woods to sing,
   And fly from tree to tree.

5. Oh let us ever humbly pray
   That grace to us be given.
   May we be ready to forgive
   That we may be forgiven.

6. When e're a task is set to you,
   Don't idly sit and view it;
   Nor be content to wish it done—
   Begin at once and do it.

7. The features may be beautiful or not
   On which we find it.
   A smile takes half its beauty from the thought
   That lies behind it.

8. To do to others as I would
   That they should do to me,
   Will make me honest, kind and good
   As children ought to be.

9. Little moments make an hour,
   Little thoughts a book,
   Little seeds, a tree or flower;
   Water drops a brook;
   Little deeds of faith and love,
   Link the earth to heaven above.

10. Be never wholly idle,
    Than which there's nothing worse,
    But read some goodly volumes
    Or even—scribble verse.

11. Speak the truth and speak it ever,
    Cost it what it will;
    He who hides the wrong he did
    Does the wrong thing still.

12. The moments fly—a minute's gone;
    The minutes fly—an hour is run;
    The day is fled—the night is here;
    Thus flies a week, a month, a year.

13. Death rides on every breeze,
    He lurks in every flower,
    Each season has its own disease,
    Its perils every hour.

14. I will not fear, for God is near,
    Through the dark night, as in the light,
    And while I sleep, safe watch will keep,
    Why should I fear, when God is near?

15. If all the good people were clever
    And all clever people were good,
    The world would be nicer than ever
    We thought that it possibly could.
    But somehow 'tis seldom or never
    The two hit it off as they should—
    The good are so harsh to the clever,
    The clever so rude to the good.

16. Don't kill the birds, the pretty birds
    That play among the trees;
    'Twould make the Earth a cheerless place
    To see no more of these.

17. There's so much good in the worst of us
    And so much bad in the best of us,
    That it ill behooves any of us
    To criticize the rest of us.

18. The child who learns to hate a lie
    And scorns to feign a false reply,
    To cover faults or errors done,
    Love and forgiveness both hath won.
    For Truth both gentle is and brave,
    But Falsehood is a coward knave,
    Who vainly tries his faults to screen
    By lying words most base and mean.

19. Tender-handed stroke a nettle,
    And it stings you for your pains;
    Grasp it like a man of mettle
    And it soft as silk remains.

20. Twelve hundred million men are spread
    About the earth and I and you
    Wonder, when you and I are dead
    What will those luckless millions do.

21. It is a sin to steal a pin,
    To borrow and not pay,
    To waste the time that is not mine,
    To cheat in any way.

22. A wise old owl lived in an oak,
    The more he saw, the less he spoke,
    The less he spoke, the more he heard—
    Why can't we be like that wise old bird?

23. A talk when you're lonely,
    A smile when you're glad,
    A help when you're weary,
    A hope when you're sad,
    A hand when you need it,
    A laugh when you're blue,
    A guide when you're searching,
    A joy all life through.

24. Life is mostly froth and bubbles,
    Two things stand like stone,
    Kindness in another's troubles,
    Courage in your own.

25. Work can make the sad light-hearted,
    Work makes strong the young and old,
    Work brings treasures far more costly
    Than the idler's gems and gold.
    All life's best has not been taken
    While "Good Work" remains to thee.
    This my wish for all my friends:
    Love and work and happy be.

26. Precious memories how they linger,
    Linger round my soul,
    In the stillness of the midnight
    Precious memories unfold.

• • •

1. From *Royal Reader*, Book 1.

2. Recorded in R.F. Sparkes's *The Winds Softly Sigh*, but taken from *Royal Reader*, Book 1.

3. From *Royal Reader*, Book 1, this verse first appeared in *Little Rhymes for Little Folk*, in the eighteenth century, according to the Opies.

4. From *Royal Reader*, Book 2.

5. From *Royal Reader*, Book 1.

6. From *Royal Reader*, Book 2.

7. *Inter Nos* (1927-34).

9. From *Royal Reader*, Book 2.

10. *Inter Nos* (1927-34).

11. *From Royal Reader*, Book 2.

12. From *Royal Reader*, Book 1.

14. *From Royal Reader*, Book 1.

15. *Inter Nos* (1927-34).

16. From *Royal Reader*, Book 3.

18. From *Royal Reader*, Book 2.

20. *Inter Nos* (1927-34).

22. The Opies report that "A Wise Old Owl" is thought to be an old rhyme, but they trace it back only to 1915 when it was quoted by John D. Rockefeller.

24. From *Among the Deep Sea Fishers* (1976), the magazine of the International Grenfell Association.

25. From *The Savour of Things Past*.

Woodsman, Spare That Tree

23. Parodies

A parody or humorous imitation of a serious work can be composed as a way of making fun of the author's effort or as a backhanded tribute to it. I think most of the parodies that circulated in Newfoundland and Labrador, particularly those of the *Royal Reader* poems, were intended as tongue-in-cheek tributes.

Parodies were quite highly regarded in our house, but I did not always recognize them for what they were. For example, when we children squabbled, Father was likely to cluck his tongue and say "Birds in their little nests agree." However, I did not know the lines by Sir Isaac Watts: "Birds in their little nests agree / And 'tis a shameful sight, / When children of one family / Fall out and chide and fight." Instead, I would silently finish with Hilaire Belloc's admonition about eating string: "Birds in the little nests agree / That breakfast, dinner, lunch and tea / Are all the human frame requires / With that the wretched child expires."

Literary parody was recognized and both enjoyed and employed at various levels by almost everyone in my family, but we were also great fans of the Canadian comedians Wayne and Shuster. Two chums from down on Fleming Street could reproduce with variations their parody of Julius Caesar, as well as other television programs such as Dragnet ("I'm Joe Friday. This is my partner, Chocolate Sundae"). Parodies of advertisements, hymns, and songs littered our lives both at school and at home, and can be found elsewhere in this collection as well as in the following sampling.

1. Woodsman, spare that tree,
   Cut not a single bough,
   It used to be Jimmy McLaughlin's
   But it's A.E. Hickman's now.

2. Woodsman, fell that tree,
   Spare not a single bough,
   For as in youth it chastised me,
   I'll not protect it now.

3. The boy stood on the burning deck
   Whence all but him had fled,
   He had Al Vardy on the air
   And Solo on his bread.

4. The boy stood on the burning deck,
   Eating peanuts by the peck.

5. The boy stood on the burning deck,
   His bum was full of blisters,
   First he wore his father's pants
   And then he wore his sister's.

6. Lives of great men oft remind us,
   As we o'er their memories turn,
   Not to die and leave behind us
   Letter that we ought to burn.

7. Holy smoke! The parson shouted,
   In the fright he lost his hair.
   Now his head is just like heaven
   For there is no parting there.

8. Church bells don't peel potatoes,
   And social bells don't ring,
   But farmer boys, they all pitch hay
   'Cause youth must have its fling.

9. When the organ peeled potatoes
   Lard was rendered by the choir,
   "Holy smoke," the preacher shouted,
   Someone's set the church on fire.

10. Thirty days hath September,
    All the rest I can't remember,
    So why bother me at all
    When there's a calendar on the wall.

11. There's no more tea for thee,
    There's no more tea for thee,
    Poor hungry soul,
    The teapot's cold,
    There's no more tea for thee.

12. Oh you must be a lover
    Of your dear grandmother,
    Or you won't get her money when she dies.

13. If you don't wear a bonnet
    With Salvation Army on it,
    You won't get to heaven when you die.

14. They told him, by golly, it couldn't be done,
    But he set his mind right to it.
    He tackled that task that couldn't be done
    And by golly, he couldn't do it.

15. To say that all is *per quippi*
    Seems to me to be silly and lippy
    The tree in the quad
    Belongs not to God,
    It's the property of C.S. Pippy.

16. Hoppin' o'er the carpet
    Picking up the crumbs,
    Peter knows the Polletts
    Feed him when he comes.

17. Daughter dear, on whom I dote,
    Send, oh send me back my coat,
    Since, if that be too much bother,
    I must go and buy another
    'Ere I face next winter's snow.
    By the breezes unconfined
    Blowing down the winter wind,
    I am rendered most forlorn
    As I go to work each morn,
    Thinking of tomorrow's snow.
    Daughter, dear! I'll cease to dote
    If you don't send back that coat!!!

18. Fish and brewis, fish and brewis,
    Tastes just like a pair of worn-out shoes,
    This I tell you, brother,
    You can't have one without the other.

19. See a pin, and let it lay,
    Your pants will hold another day.

20. Tom, Tom, the piper's son,
    Picked up a girl and had some fun.

21. Turn backward, turn backward, oh time in thy flight,
    And make me a child, Lord, just for tonight,
    Make me a child as I'm travelling to Ayr
    And being a child, Lord, I'll travel half fare.

22. I'm Popeye the sailor man,
    I live in a garbage can,
    I eats all the lizards
    And spits out their gizzards,
    I'm Popeye the sailor man.

1-2. These are parodies of "Woodsman spare that tree, / Touch not a single bough, / In youth it sheltered me / And I'll protect it now," by George P. Morris, 1802-1864. Recorded by Fred Adams.

3-5. Parodies of the poem "Casabianca" by Mrs. Felicia Dorothea Hemans, which begins "The boy stood on the burning deck." Al Vardy was radio spokesman for Solo margarine.

6. A parody of "Lives of great men all remind us / We can make our lives sublime, / And, departing, leave behind us, / Footprints on the sands of time," from "The Psalm of Life." From Gordon Williams.

7. From Les Harris, *Growing Up with Verse.*

8. From Gordon Williams.

9. A parody of "When the Organ Played at Twilight," from Gordon Williams.

10. Parody of the mnemonic that begins the same way (see section 8 verse 11).

11. A gently, mocking version of "There's mercy still for thee, / There's mercy still for thee, / Poor trembling soul / He'll make thee whole, / There's mercy still for thee."

12-13. "Oh you must be a lover of the Lord, / Or you won't get to heaven when you die." The version about the bonnet came from Judy Norman in Sheshatshiu.

14. This verse was originally "Somebody said that it couldn't be done / But he with a chuckle replied, / That maybe it couldn't, but he would be one / Who wouldn't say so till he'd tried." This parody came from Gordon Williams.

15. "To say that all is *per quippi*" is a parody of the many responses to Bishop Berkeley's conundrum, "If a tree falls in the forest and no one

hears it, did it really fall?" The best known of these is "There was a young man who said 'God / Must think it exceedingly odd / If he finds that this tree / Continues to be / When there's no one about in the Quad,'" which elicited the reply "Dear sir, your astonishment's odd / I am always about in the Quad / And that's why the tree / Continues to be, / Since observed by yours faithfully, God." The Newfoundland version was composed in the 1960s when Ches Pippy was buying up land behind the university to develop Pippy Park.

16. "Hoppin' o'er the Carpet" is a parody of "Welcome Robin" from the *Royal Readers*. This comes from Ron Pollett.

17. "Daughter Dear, on Whom I Dote" is a parody of Lord Byron's "Maid of Athens," addressed by my father to my sister Leslie.

18. "Fish and Brewis" was sung to the tune of "Love and Marriage," and I remember hearing the London Players sing it.

19. "See a Pin and Let It Lay" is a parody of "See a Pin and Pick It Up," composed by Tommy Wilansky when he was a boy in the 1930s.

20. This parody of the English nursery rhyme was on the go in 1966 when I started at Memorial.

21. A parody of "Rock Me to Sleep," by Elizabeth Akers Allen, 1860.

22. With the introduction of television to Newfoundland in the 1950s, we became familiar with a whole new culture of parodies. The original Popeye song went, "I'm strong to the finish / Cause I eats my spinach," and ended, "So keep good behaver / That's your one life saver." We sang about lizards and also "I eats all the worms / And I spits out the germs." The Davy Crockett song "Born on a Mountaintop in Tennessee" became "Born in a Taxicab in New York City," and the Superman opening "It's a bird, it's a plane, it's Superman" became "It's a bird, it's a plane, (mime wiping bird doo out of your eye) it's a bird!"

Uncle Joe Drover

24. People

I had always thought that nursery rhyme figures, such as the see-sawing Margery Dawe and the dusty Polly Flinders, were ordinary people. It was rather disappointing to discover that Jack Spratt is a sixteenth-century term for a dwarf and that Robin the Bobbin was thought to be a reference to Henry VIII. I preferred the idea that every-day men and women had found immortality in our childhood verses. It was a relief to discover that, in Newfoundland, they had.

My oldest brother, Seumas, was a character in a town replete with characters. He wasn't deformed or mad or wicked, like the odd figures that Jack Fitzgerald and Fred Adams have written about, but he was a bit slow and he danced to his own drummer. He worked at various labouring jobs when he could find them, and usually kept himself busy and out of trouble by maintaining a regular round of walks and visits around town.

Seumas specialized in collecting little bits of gossip that he traded like currency, and had the knack of being funny without cruelty or crudity. He knew he was a bit different, and that sometimes worried him, but as often as not he liked standing out from the crowd. I was always surprised to hear shopkeepers call him *Mister* McGrath, but he had a strong sense of his own worth, and he had decided that form of address sat well on him.

I've always thought the people whose names turn up in local rhymes must have been a good bit like Seumas, ordinary people who had a particular way about them that made them memorable. Not long after Seumas died, I ran into an old friend who had a sister who was a lot like my brother. His sister is kept on a very short leash, very close to home. "Seumas was so lucky," he told me. "He had the run of the town and he had friends, everybody knew him. He had such a full life." I don't know that I'd go so far as to say he was lucky, but it could have been a lot worse for him and I wonder if he's immortalized in a verse I haven't found yet.

1. I went up to Ferryland, saw an old woman,
   Sweeten her tea with a rake,
   Then I went on and I saw Johnny Jordan
   Go down to his ears in the flake.

2. Now Mickey Fling, the railway king, your duty you must do,
   If you don't do your duty from the Topsails you'll skidoo,
   You're shoveling snow just like a crow, I hear the people say,
   If you don't be more attentive and let your work be seen,
   We'll send you back as an exile to live in Skivereen.

3. Sister Philomena went aboard a steamer,
   The steamer sunk and she got drunk
   And that was the end of Sister Philomena.

4. Who's that walking down the street,
   Mrs. Simpson's dirty feet,
   She's got Edward by the hand,
   Acting like an old cowhand.
   God have mercy on that dame,
   She just took our king for fame.

5. There once was a king and his name was Ned,
   He sat upon the throne and said
   To hell with the crown, I'll heave it down,
   And I'll marry Mrs. Simpson instead.

6. Oh mister skate from the angry deep,
   I won't cause your friends to weep,
   But when you go to your home below,
   Tell them Tom Howlett let you go.

7. Uncle Joe Drover from Island Cove came,
   With his hatchet, his hammer, his chisel and plane,
   The wind from the westward, it came on to blow,
   And Uncle Joe Drover got bogged in the snow.

8. Dear Mr. Belbin, I know he's all right,
   He labours quite hard both by day and by night.
   Keeping things straight with the boys on the job,
   And his neat little coaker stuck up on his knob.

9. There was a hard-swearing old sailor
   Whose language would frighten a jailer,
   But he freely averred
   That Peg Godden, when stirred,
   Would startle the crew of a whaler.

10. There was hurdy-gurdy Mick
    And hurdy-gurdy Lar
    And hurdy-gurdy Marks and Dan
    And Myles and Tom and Ger.

11. Old Nicky Putt with his hutty-tut-tut,
    Said the wharf should be put o'er in The Gut.
    But old Uncle Noah gave a hell of a roar,
    And said the wharf should be o'er where it was before.

12. Two and four are something more
    Than three and three can be,
    Two is Aiden, four is Misha,
    I am thirty-three.
    Mama is the same as me
    And that makes sixty-six,
    And so between the two of us
    We're wise to all your tricks.

13. Coming up from Broad Cove
    To make the devil laugh,
    Andy on the tailboard
    Sylvie on the shaft,
    Arthur with the scrubbing brush
    Scrubbing out his ears.

14. Never yet has history shown
    A cleric on a royal throne,
    But here we see before we stand
    A Parson, king of Baffin land.

15. Up with the kettle
    Down with the pan,
    Mary Joe Brothers
    And Dinny and Dan.

16. Jim Tuff he builds dories,
    And he builds 'em neat and strong,
    While his brother Tom hunts rabbits
    And he hunts them all day long.

17. There's another elt in the harbour,
    John Mitchell is his name
    And when the wind is at its height
    He says it's getting calm.

18. Good morning to your worship,
    Good morning to Judge Prowse,
    May flights of little angels
    Fly about your house.

19. Peter Penton he came down,
    All dressed up neat and dandy,
    He swore that he'd get Lizzie Burke,
    Or otherwise Til Sandy.

20. Anyone here seen Tobin?
    T.O.B.I.N.
    Is there anybody here seen Tobin?
    You'd know him by his grin.
    His hair is red and his eyes are blue,
    He is Irish through and through.
    Is there anybody here seen Tobin?
    Tobin in the motorboat.

21. Roman Bill
    Lived on the hill,
    And if he's not dead
    He's living there still.

22. On Friday last at half past two, two love bestricken chaps
  Up in Fort Townsend Hollow met for satisfactory raps.
  One of them Gus Healey was, the other Dooley Din,
  Come over here from Heart's Content, Miss –'s green heart to win.
  John Sullivan the bobby fop, turned six policemen out,
  And wheeled to the pistolizing sound, right around to the left about.
  With pistols lowered beneath their arms, they hied to Casey's farm,
  Where Dooley Din got well oiled off behind John Casey's barn.

• • •

1. Johnny Jordan was a well-known character on the Southern Shore. Wayne Ledwell explained that a man from Calvert made up this rhyme to make fun of him because you only go through the flake if you are careless or it is badly made. The first lines about the woman sweetening her tea with a rake establishes the nonsensical nature of what happened to Johnny Jordan.

2. Mickey Flynn, a native of Skivereen, was section foreman at The Quarry on the Gaff Topsails. This verse was made up by the telegraph operator, and recorded by Tom Quilliam in *Look 'Ere Me Son*.

4. Wallis Simpson was the American divorcee that King Edward, later Duke of Windsor, gave up the throne to marry. This verse comes from Tom Dawe's *The Yarns of Ishmael Drake*.

5. From George Riche of Rigolet, printed in Tim Borlase's *Songs of Labrador*.

8. This "Rhyme of the Hunchback" was composed when Mr. Belbin was working as timekeeper as the government wharf was being built in St. Philip's after the old one was taken out by an iceberg. It was said that Belbin, the schoolmaster in the winter, had one arm twice the size of the other from beating the children. The verse was recorded by Bob Tucker. I believe a "coaker" was a hat similar to that worn by the founder of the Fisherman's Protective Union.

9. Margaret Frances Godden was a lifetime civil servant. She retired as Assistant Deputy Minister of the Department of Development. The verse was written by my father, J.M.F. McGrath.

10. From John Carrick Greene in *Of Fish and Family*.

11. Nicky Putt from Brigus argued that the new government wharf should be in Brigus Harbour, while Noah Clarke believed it should be in Riverhead where the old wharf had been. This verse was recorded for me by Wayne Spracklin.

12. This verse was made up by my son, Eli Gedalof, for the amusement of his sons Misha and Aiden. Misha, who was four at the time, was just becoming aware of the various ages of members of his family.

13. The people coming from Broad Cove were Squires from St. Philip's. The verse came from Gerrie Pellegrinetti, at the museum in Torbay.

14. Ralph Parsons was a Hudson's Bay company manger in Baffin Island. The verse was recorded by Jack Hambling in *The Second Time Around: Growing Up in Bay Roberts*. It is also quoted in *The King of Baffin Island* by John Parsons and Burton K. Janes, who say it was written by Michael Lubbock.

15. Dale Jarvis, in *Wonderful Strange: Ghosts, Fairies and Fabulous Beasties*, records this as an addition to the Wren Boys' song from Renews.

16. From Otto Kelland in *Dories and Dorymen*.

17. An "elt" is a sleeveen or scoundrel. From the *Dictionary of Newfoundland English*.

18. By "the poet of Pokeham Path," as recorded by George Story in the *Dictionary of Canadian Biography XIV*.

19. A dance rhyme, recorded by John Carrick Greene in *Of Fish and Family*.

20. From Aunt Gertrude Chubbs, Battle Harbour region, recorded in *Linking the Generations*, edited by Bonnie Rumbolt.

21. "Roman Bill" was Bill Tucker, who converted and married a Catholic. His son, also called Roman Bill, still lives on Tucker's Hill in St. Philip's.

22. This verse is about two lovesick cable operators from the Heart's Content Cable Station. On September 5, 1873, Gus Healey challenged Dennis Dooley to a duel. Dooley, who fainted before the pistols were fired, took a beating and the girl refused both of them. The verse is recorded in *I Have Touched the Greatest Ship* by Melvin Rowe.

Little Willie in Bows and Sashes

25. Humour

Quite a lot has been written about Newfoundland humour, which is distinctly different from Canadian humour. Labrador humour is in a category of its own, and, as far as I know, nobody claims to know anything about it at all, except that it exists. The most common take on what we Newfoundlanders find funny is that it is a survival mechanism made necessary by our bad weather.

Nothing could have been further from my idea of Newfoundland humour than the ubiquitous "Newfie" joke as it was known in Toronto. Much of our humour was self-deprecating, but with a twist. Typical of the kind of humour I grew up with is the joke about a fellow with a B.A. in English from Memorial, who was looking for a job on a construction site. When the foreman charged him with not knowing the difference between a joist and a girder, he indignantly responded that "Joist was an Irishman who wrote dirty books, and Girder was a German poet."

A sense of humour was not only helpful in getting along in our chaotic household, it was absolutely essential. However, storytelling and wit were appreciated more than the ability to tell a joke. This isn't to say jokes weren't appreciated, but they were considered fluff, one-day wonders that could not usually bear a second telling. Comic verses tended to fall into that category, with exceptions made for Lear, Belloc, and Ogden Nash.

The following selection is a rather mixed bag, an accurate reflection of the random nature of comic verses that circulated when I was a youth. Several of the offerings come from my father's pen, and several are English and American imports. The really funny Newfoundland and Labrador material is to be found all through this collection, not just in this one section.

1. Little Willie hung his sister,
   She was dead before we missed her.
   Willie's always up to tricks—
   Ain't he cute? He's only six.

2. Little Willie in bows and sashes,
   Fell in the fire and got burned to ashes.
   In the winter when the weather is chilly,
   No one likes to poke poor Willie.

3. Baby Billy in the tub,
   Ma forgot to put in the plug,
   Oh what sorrow, oh what pain,
   There goes Billy down the drain.

4. There was an old woman
   And what do you think,
   She lived upon nothing
   But vittles and drink,
   Vittles and drink
   Were the chief of her diet,
   And yet that old woman
   Would never be quiet.

5. I love life and life loves me,
   I'm as happy as can be,
   A happier man nowhere exists—
   I think I'll go and slash my wrists.

6. Last night as I sat on the stair
   I saw a man who wasn't there;
   He wasn't there again today—
   I wish to heck he'd go away.

7. A woman who fasted for sixty-two days,
   To see if the stunt could be done,
   From hundreds of Scotsmen had letters of praise
   And proposals from seventy-one.

8. Some people like art,
   But myself I like money.
   The knave liked a tart
   (Some people like art
   Or pressed duck *à la carte*)
   But such choices seem funny!
   Some people like art
   But myself, I like money.

9. This is the story of Willie McGuire,
   Who ran down the street with his pants on fire.
   He ran to the doctor in a terrible fright,
   And the doctor said, "Willie, your end is in sight."

10. There was an old person whose habits,
    Inclined him to feed upon rabbits,
    When he'd eaten eighteen,
    He turned perfectly green,
    That old man with the bad habits.

11. The last time I sent you a dollar
    You never said "thank you" at all.
    I thought with delight you would holler,
    The last time I sent you a dollar,
    So now with another I'll foller
    But you'd better prepare for a squall—
    It's the last time I'll send you a dollar
    If you never say "thank you" at all.

12. There was a man in our town,
    And he was wondrous wise,
    He jumped into a bramble bush
    And scratched out both his eyes,
    But when he saw his eyes were out,
    With all his might and main,
    He jumped into another bush
    And scratched them in again.

13. Where was Moses when the lights went out?
    Down in the cellar with his shirt tail out.

14. Janet playing in the street,
    Careless was and indiscreet,
    And her head with nothing filled,
    By a car was nearly killed.
    Goodness, that would be a shame—
    Daddy'd miss his poker game.

15. Jack the Ripper stole a kipper,
    Hid it in his father's slipper.

16. I'd rather have a touten
    Than do without 'en.

17. Timothy Thompson
    Fell out of bed rompsin'
    And banged his head on the floor.
    Now Timothy Thompson
    Don't go rompsin'
    Any more.

18. Poppy Dick, Poppy Dick,
    Put your foot down quick,
    Kick your legs up high,
    Point your finger to the sky.

19. Pork and cabbage all the year,
    Mouldy bread and sour beer,
    Rusty bacon, stinky cheese.
    A damp bed full of fleas—
    Who do you think would live here?

20. I love you once, I love you mighty,
    I wish my pajamas were next to your nighty.
    Don't take insult to what I have said,
    I mean on the clothesline, not on the bed.

21. Tomorrow's the fair,
    And I will be there,
    Stuffing my guts
    With gingerbread nuts.

22. Father's gone around the bay
    To get a load of cotton,
    If he don't bring the flowerdy stuff,
    I hope he don't bring nuttin'.

23. I have a tie rack full of ties
    Narrow and wide and every size,
    Striped and plain and polka-dotted,
    Silk and rayon, clean and spotted.
    Yes, I have ties of every kind,
    Ties subdued and ties that blind,
    Ties that dazzle and ties that scare,
    And also the two I always wear.

24. The elephant is a pretty bird
    It flits from bough to bough,
    It builds its nest in a rhubarb tree
    And whistles like a cow.

• • •

1-2. The Little Willie verses came, originally, from *Ruthless Rhymes for Heartless Homes*, written by Harry Graham (1898). I remember variations on at least a half dozen of these amusingly grotesque quatrains, although I was unaware that they all originated with the same author.

3. "Baby Billy," written in the style of "Little Willie," was recorded by Anne Morris, a grade nine student at Henry Gordon Academy in Cartwright in *Labradorite*, II, a 1970 yearbook.

4. The Opies trace this verse, a favourite of my family, back to 1784.

5. I recall hearing this verse first in 1966 at Memorial.

6. Written by Hughes Mearns as "Antigonish" in 1899, this variation was sent to me by Gordon Williams.

7. From Ivan F. Jesperson's *Fat-Back and Molasses*.

8. Written by my father, J.M.F. McGrath.

10. Recorded by John Blake of North West River.

11. Written by my father, J.M.F. McGrath.

12. The Opies date this verse about a man from Thessaly back to the 1760s. This version was recorded by Sam Morris, a grade seven student at Henry Gordon Academy, Cartwright, Labrador.

13. The usual answer to the question is "In the dark." This variant was sent to me by Gordon Williams.

14. Written by my father, J.M.F. McGrath, about my sister Janet Kelly. This is a good example of how black humour is used to deal with traumatic events. When she was very small, shortly after they moved to town from Harbour Grace, Janet was hit by a car. Bruised but not badly hurt, she ran home and hid behind the sofa, thinking she would get into trouble for having been in the street. She fell asleep in hiding and was missing for several hours, while the family, alerted by the driver, searched frantically for her, thinking she might have had a concussion and be dying. A "Heartless Homes" style rhyme resulted.

17. From Ron Young in the *Downhome*. "Rompsing" or "rampsing" is not a word I was familiar with until I heard it used repeatedly in a rather bizarre sexual assault trial in Cartwright. I think I was the only person in the room who didn't know it meant goofing around or "romping."

18. Recorded by Albert Holmes in *A Boat of My Own*.

21. From Les Harris in *Growing Up with Verse*.

22. From Clyde Scott in *A History of Little Bay East, Fortune Bay*.

23. From Leander Rowsell in *An Energetic Newfoundlander*.

24. From *Folk Speech*, Book I, by John Widdowson.

I Know the Ethie *Is No Use*

26. Ships and Boats

In Newfoundland and Labrador, people have an affection for boats and ships that tends to attach itself to particular vessels. I grew up with the names of certain ships ringing in my ears. It had always been a source of some pride that my mother's family came over from England and Ireland to Lord Baltimore's settlement in Ferryland in the 1500s on either the *Dove* or the *Ark of Avalon*. My maternal grandfather's grandfather, Michael Kearney, was a famous shipbuilder who designed and constructed the *Rothesay, Thomas Ridley, Shamrock,* and other well-known ships. When he prepared to launch the *Ida,* he hung his pocket-watch on the inside of a brick archway through which she had to pass, to prove he'd calculated her width correctly. A great deal of money was lost and won that day as she sailed gently down the slipway, clearing the arch and the watch by inches.

As a young man my father signed on to the *Terra Nova* for his first sealing voyage. That was the ship which took Scott to the Antarctic. My Grandfather Kearney narrowly missed drowning on the *Florizel,* a fate that the father of a family friend did not escape. One of my brothers later went to The Front aboard the *Algerine* and at least one brother and a sister served on the hospital ship *Lady Anderson*.

There were dozens of other ships whose names I heard all around me— *Caribou, Gilleanes, Christmas Seal,* and the ferries *John Guy, Beaumont Hamel, NONIA, Joseph and Clara Smallwood*. Up in Labrador, I would hear about the *Harmony, Kyle, Yale, Bowdoin, Maraval,* and, in recent years, the *Northern Ranger,* and the *Bond*.

Many of these ships I never saw but they were as real to me as the photos of relatives in our family albums. One ship in particular became part of my life for a time, when I was doing research one summer at the Scott Polar Research Institute in Cambridge, England. The *Terra Nova*'s bell was installed in a little nook on the stairs at the institute, and at tea time an archivist would go and solemnly ring it to let her colleagues know it was time to knock off for fifteen minutes. Each time, I thought of my father and of the whaling the bell must have gotten when it was being rung to call the sealers back from the ice.

1. All naval ships have had their time,
   But there's one in particular that's a ship of the line,
   For most ships in their day have a story to tell,
   But for some all that's left is their name on a bell.

2. Oh boundless starvation,
   The bay's full of ice.
   We have no tobacco,
   No tea and no rice.
   The *Clyde*'s stuck in Lewisporte,
   She's there for to stay,
   We needs a sou'wester
   To clear out the bay.

3. Travelling in the *Primrose* in Notre Dame Bay,
   Travelling in the *Primrose*; our captain knows the way,
   Travelling in the darkness at the close of day,
   We shall anchor safely in the Harbour.

4. Salt herring fresh from Fortune Bay,
   Come this week by the schooner *May*;
   If you don't want them for your dinner,
   You can have them for your tay.

5. I know the *Ethie* is no use,
   For every bolt and screw is loose.
   I know she'll go down like the *Bruce*
   And drown poor Newfoundlanders.

6. The judge said, "Up hinders,
   And pin back your ears,
   You're sentenced to the *Meigle*
   For twenty-one years."

7. She made them sick, she made them green,
   She made them reek of kerosene,
   But of all ships in steam or sail,
   There's none to be compared to *Yale*.

8. Farewell to the good ship *Iceland*,
   The wealth she brought was great
   Although she's gone to Davy Jones
   Thank God her crew are safe.

9. Come all ye bully northern men,
   For trunks we have no use;
   We'll pack our rags in canvas bags
   And go aboard the *Bruce*.

10. The *Tancook*'s in the harbour
    Johnny Manning at the wheel,
    Every time she strikes a lop
    You can see her crooked keel.

11. It's the set of the sails
    And not the gales
    Which tell us the way to go.

12. First he primed her then he timed her,
    Threw the wheel over and she would not go.
    Then he burned off the oil and examined the coil,
    The nuts were off and he did not know.

13. There's no ship that's been built,
    Who's slipped out on a tide,
    That can boast quite so much,
    Nor fill men with such pride,
    When this Colony Class Cruiser,
    With its Blue Jacket Band
    Took her name on the slip-way
    From St. John's, *Newfoundland*.

14. There was a young man named Johnny Magory
    Went into the woods to build a new dory,
    When he came back his mother was dead
    And three little babbies sat up in the bed.

15. George Pope is a fine looking fellow,
    On Sundays he dresses in brown,
    He fishes with Captain Sid Harris,
    In the *Pauline C. Winters* he's found.

16. It's to me Johnny Poker
    We'll haul up this heavy joker,
    And it's to me Johnny Poker
    Haul—ha—haul—ha!

17. Pull me Jolly Poker,
    An we'll haul and pull together,
    And 'tis do me Jolly Poker
    Haul!

18. Rango was a sailor,
    He shipped on board a whaler,
    Rango, boys, Rango.

19. Haul on the bowline,
    Haul and bust the towline,
    Haul on the bowline,
    Haul, boys, haul.

20. Eloquent, though all unheard,
    Swiftly speeds the secret word,
    Light and dark or foul and fair,
    Still a message prompt to bear;
    None can read it on the way,
    None its unseen transit stay.

21. Haul on the bowline,
    The bugger must come this time,
    Haul on the bowline,
    Haul, boys, haul.

22. Saturday's sail
    Will never fail.

23. When I'm a man I means to be
    A carpenter, as you will see.
    I'll hammer with a busy hand
    And build the best boats in Newfoundland.

24. One night a lady named Banker
    Sailing to Casablanca,
    Awoke in dismay
    To hear the mate say,
    Hoist up the top sheets and spanker.

25. In Grady's Harbour I went one time,
    I bought a punt from old man Ryan.
    The sea hove in, she caught a ground,
    I lost my punt which cost a pound.

26. The *Pill Box*'s pennant is now flying in the breeze,
    The *Pill Box* is launched to sail on fair or stormy seas,
    The *Pill Box* is ready to bring health to all disease,
    At the good old P.I.H.

• • •

1. Written by 'Shipmate' Malcolm Brown, published by Keith Collier in the *Newfoundland Quarterly* (2007).

2. This parody of "Oh Boundless Salvation" came from Otto Tucker in the *Newfoundland Quarterly* (Winter 1990), but Sue Jones claimed in the *Downhome* that her father, from Moreton's Harbour, wrote the verse.

3. This is probably another parody of a hymn, and I believe it also originated with Otto Tucker, possibly recorded by Cyril Poole.

4. From Fred Adams, and also in Jack Fitzgerald's *Newfoundland Fireside Stories*.

5. The *Ethie* and the *Bruce* are part of the Alphabet Fleet, coastal vessels of the Reid-Newfoundland Railway. The *Ethie* sank on December 10, 1919, near Cow Head. The 90 passengers and crew were all landed safely on shore via a boatswain's chair.

6. The *Meigle*, also a part of the Alphabet Fleet, was used as a prison ship for a short while after the dole riots of 1932. This verse came from Paul O'Neill's *The Oldest City*.

7. The *Yale* was a Grenfell mission ship, named for the university where many of her volunteers studied. The verse comes from *Among the Deep Sea Fishers* (1980).

8. The *Iceland* verse comes from Shannon Ryan's *The Ice Hunters*. A steamer of 287 tons burthen, *The Iceland* joined the St. John's sealing fleet in 1872.

9. This verse was on a Gerald S. Doyle Christmas card in a series called "The Good Old Ships of Newfoundland" and was reprinted in Maura Hanrahan's *The Alphabet Fleet*.

10. From Les Harris's *Growing Up with Verse*. A reader has suggested that the *Tancook* was probably a Nova Scotia vessel.

11. From the *Downhome* (2003).

12. From Mary Francis Coady, the *Downhome* (2003), about the first gas engines, introduced in about 1915.

13. From Keith Collier in the *Newfoundland Quarterly* (2007).

14. A magory was a rosehip, and Johnny Magory is a common nursery rhyme figure. I confess, this is one of the few verses I bowdlerized as, in the original version I found, it wasn't "babbies" that were found in the bed but one of the two "N" words that I dislike so much. This verse came from the *Dictionary of Newfoundland English*.

15. From Greta Hussey, *Our Life on Lear's Room, Labrador*.

16-17. This is a variation on the shanties or hauling songs called Johnny Pokers or Jolly Pokers. There are dozens of versions in different communities.

18. From P.K. Devine's *In the Good Old Days*.

20. From the *Dictionary of Newfoundland English*.

21. A tribute to the four cables laid by the *Great Eastern* for the Heart's Content cable station, quoted in *I Have Touched the Greatest Ship* by Melvin Rowe.

22. This is an injunction never to launch a boat on a Friday, from Nellie Strowbridge's *The Newfoundland Tongue*.

23. This is a Christmas concert recitation from La Scie, 1942, from Otto Tucker's *That Nothing Be Lost*.

25. From *Folk Ballads and Songs of the Labrador Coast*, by MacEdward Leach. Grady Harbour, which is sometimes rendered as "Greedy Harbour," is near Cartwright.

26. The motor boat *Pill Box* was christened July 12, 1912, at Pilley's Island for the Pilley's Island Hospital. Quoted by Dennis Gill, *Newfoundland Quarterly* (Winter 1984), p. 20.

La Scie, That's We

27. Place Names

A great deal is made of the unusual place names of Newfoundland and Labrador. To those of us who live here, however, the names Dildo or Old Shop, Butter and Snow, or Mulligan conjure up a vast array of associations, and very few guffaws. Ron Seary, writing in *Place Names of the Avalon*, reminds us that "to know the meaning of a name is to endow it with greater significance," which perhaps explains why the name, divorced from the place itself, fails to raise a laugh among Newfoundlanders.

During my idyllic sojourn in Beachy Cove, I became quite fascinated with the local names, like Horse's Drink, Dead Calf Ridge, and Top of the World, because I was always trying to find my way around in the woods. My back meadow was called "The Bonus," according to local lore, because you could coast a sled for a full mile from the top down to Drummer's Hole on a good winter day. Others have told me that the meadow was the government bonus for the original settlers having cleared a specified number of acres of land. "The Geeze," over the ferry dock, was so called either for the Portuguese sailors buried there by Gaspar Corte-Real or because it was a "gaze," a high point of land suitable for spotting ships and seabirds.

Newfoundlanders, like Inuit, name places on the ocean as well as on the land. The Trap Berth Registry for the waters I could see from my bedroom window included names such as Place Where the Man Fell Over (where one of the Hammonds fell into the sea while carrying a barrel of flour alongside a cliff), Stem and Stern, and Mike and All's Cook Room (where Mike Reardigan and his crew used to stop for their breakfast).

These verses don't explain place names but they do use them. This was one way of personalizing rhymes to make them local. For example, when I was looking for Labrador examples, I was offered "Going to Porcupine."

Porcupines aren't found in Newfoundland but are common in Labrador. However, I'd heard a variation on the same verse years earlier in Torbay, "Going down to Broad Cove," where the targets were riding a long cart, not a komatik. I was told in detail the exact circumstances under which the verse was composed and who exactly the family names referred to but I've no doubt the Labrador versifier could have done the same thing. Clearly, the place name verses invite adaptation and are a way of planting the flag of ownership on a verse.

1. Four days in Hooping Harbour
   We were being delayed,
   When down 'board the schooner
   Comes a fair pretty maid.

2. Old horse, old horse,
   What brings you here,
   From Sable Island
   To Carbonear?

3. Harbour Grace is a hungry place,
   And so is Carbonear,
   But when you come to old Bell Isle
   You're sure to get your share.

4. Fortune gullies and Grand Bank shags,
   All tied up in wrapper bags,
   When the bags began to bust,
   The Fortune gullies began to cuss.

5. There's a vessel up in Dildo,
   And another in Old Shop,
   But the one that's up in Dildo,
   She is turned bottom up.

6. The wolf is gone to Muddy Bay
   And won't be back 'til break of day—
   May all your sheep come home.

7. Going to Porcupine
   To make the people laugh,
   Betsy on the komatik
   And Ben between the shafts.

8. Give three cheers for Shango Bay,
   Hip, hip, hip hooray.

9. Shearstown Tigers—
   Who are dey?
   Big white bunnies
   Stuffed wit hay.

10. Whenever you meet a Branch man,
    Just ask 'em what's their name,
    If it's English, Power or Mooney,
    Treat 'em with disdain.

11. Penneys, Powells,
    Pikes and Howells—
    That was Carbonear.

12. One, two, three,
    Believe in we,
    One, two, three,
    La Scie, that's we.

13. A simple old soul from Cow Head,
    Whose children were crying for bread,
    Said, we can't risk the onus
    Of taking the Bonus—
    We'll eat Letters Patent instead.

14. We are the boys from Casey Lane,
    At night time we have fun,
    For when a policeman shows his nose
    Up Flower Hill we run.

We stand behind the coffin house,
We don't know snow or rain,
There's none coop up a corner
Like the boys from Casey's Lane.

15. Going to Topsail,
    Married for to be,
    A little drop of lassie
    And a little bit of tea,
    Here comes Connolly,
    Kicking at the rocks,
    Looking for a hatchet
    To beat up Sally's box.

16. Harbour Grace and Carbonear,
    Take I there, take I there.

17. Bonjour, Monsieur,
    Welcome here,
    And good cheer
    At St. Pierre.

18. Perlican girls are snappy,
    Winterton girls are smart,
    But it takes a girl from old St. John's
    To really win your heart.

19. Give us a place we can play,
    So we're not in the street every day,
    The sidewalks are dirty, the glass is too sharp,
    There's too many sailors in Bannerman Park,
    They're waiting to grab us as soon as it's dark.

20. Very well done, said Johnny Brown,
    Is this the way to St. John's town?
    One foot up and one foot down,
    That's the way to St. John's town.

21. The praties is so small in Green's Harbour,
    The praties is so small in Green's Harbour,
    The praties is so small when they digs 'em in the fall,
    That they eats 'em skins and all in Green's Harbour.

22. Looking out over Spreadeagle Bay,
    Dildo's content with being risqué.

23. Where are you going, you silly old man,
    With your dogs and your tacklin'?
    I'm going to Lassy Crock Hill,
    To get a load of green starrigan.

24. No visitor should leave until
    They've seen the view from old Gun Hill;
    Each way you turn presents a new
    And perfect panoramic view.

25. Hollow road, rocky road,
    Point La Haye to Sandy,
    Gaskiers is the dirty hole,
    St. Mary's is the dandy.

• • •

1. From Aubrey Tizzard in *On Sloping Ground*.

2. I have heard this verse refer to both Carbonear and Belvedere. Salt horse was old, tough salt beef. The traditional sailor's address to his salt beef goes "Salt horse, salt horse, what brought you here, / You've carried turf for many a year, / From Dublin quay to Ballyoch / You've carried turf upon your back."

3. Quoted by Gail Weir in *The Miners of Wabana*. A variant is "Harbour Grace is a hungry place, / And Carbonear is not much better, / So you've got to go to old Bell Isle / To get your bread and butter."

4. Sometimes this verse says "All wrapped up in paper bags." Gulls and shags are seabirds, which is presumably where the names come from.

Boys from Fortune told me that when they visited Grand Bank, local boys would shout "Gully, gully, gully!" at them across the street.

5. From Ron Pollett in *The Ocean at My Doorstep*.

6. Muddy Bay is near Cartwright, Labrador. I originally found this verse in *Them Days*, but children in Cartwright told me it was part of a hide-and-seek game.

7. From Greta Hussey in *Our Life on Lear's Room, Labrador*.

8. There were two more lines to this verse, which was made up by the children of Davis Inlet, but I didn't catch them. I heard it in the background of a CBC radio program on the ceremonies opening the new community of Natuashish.

10. From the late P.J. Murray of Murray's Pond, Portugal Cove.

11. From Flora Penney Head of Pondside, Carbonear, 2005.

12. From Rory Labert on CBC radio's "Madly Off in All Directions."

13. Thought to be written by Greg Power as part of his pro-confederate propaganda campaign for J.R. Smallwood. Published in the *Books of Newfoundland*, Vol. 5.

14. This verse appeared in the *Evening Chronicle* in 1907.

15. From Greta Hussey in *Our Life on Lear's Room, Labrador*.

16. From John Joy. My version is "Come by 'ere, come by 'ere." George Whiteley records it as "Me eyeballs they grows loose / When I thinks I sees the *Bruce*; / Harbour Grace and Carbonear, / Take I there, oh take I there."

17. From the *Harbour Grace Standard*, 1883.

18. By Jeff Bursey, *Globe and Mail*, March 2007.

19. Probably by Ron Hynes, from Chris Brookes's history of the Mummers Troupe, *A Public Nuisance*.

20. The first two lines of this verse appear in the *Dictionary of Newfoundland English*.

21. From Ron Pollett, *The Ocean at My Door*, as well as elsewhere. I read somewhere that this was a well-known Irish famine song, adapted to Newfoundland place names.

23. From Clementine Dalton Frampton of Goose Bay, formerly of Little Catalina.

24. Gun Hill is in Trinity, from *Aspects of the History of Trinity* by Rev. Edmund Hunt, edited by Percy Janes.

25. From *Folk Speech*, Book I, by John Widdowson.

Put Your Two Cigarettes In

28. Celebrating the Vices

I t is commonly understood that folk verses are vehicles for socially unacceptable views, scatological humour, racist or sexist attitudes, and otherwise shocking or wicked opinions. It's little wonder, then, that many of them explore the joys and difficulties associated with two popular vices, smoking and drinking. Naturally, for every bad boy or girl who celebrated the vices, there was a good boy or girl to condemn them. This selection presents both sides of the controversy.

As a reformed smoker and an unreformed tippler, I have leaned both ways at times. When I was a child, I associated tobacco and alcohol with sociability and adventure. Beer was the family business, and I loved the smell of the hops that wafted up from our rival brewery on Circular Road. We used to line up for hours to collect plastic hop bags, which could be washed out and sold for anything from a nickel to a quarter to the housewives in the neighbourhood.

Both my parents gave up smoking before I was born, which didn't stop each and every one of their children from taking up cigarettes for a time. Rationally, I know it is a disgusting habit, but the scent of tobacco smoke drifting through a spruce woods in summer is enough to send a jolt of nostalgia for the weed through me, more than three decades since my last draw.

When other girls were dreaming about being Annette Funicello or Brenda Lee, I wanted a kilt and bonnet like the girl on the Macdonald's cigarette package. My favourite uncle worked at the tobacco factory, and he always had wonderful stories about the other workers and the salesmen. Furthermore, I associated the Imperial Tobacco wooden water tower so closely with inner-city St. John's that the day they took it down I thought the world was coming to an end.

Now, having seen a number of friends and relatives drink and smoke themselves into the next world, I am rather relieved that children are being made aware of the dangers of overindulgence. I collected the counting-out rhyme "Put your two cigarettes in" from a young friend in Harbour Main who used the opportunity to give her father a veiled scolding for the occasional cigarette he still indulges in. I'm with her on this one—the non-starter is smarter.

1. When you are married
   And have children happy,
   I hope that every one of them
   Will chew tobaccy!

2. Don't ever marry an old man,
   I'll tell you the reason why,
   His lips are all tobacco juice
   And his chin is never dry
   For an old man he is old,
   For an old man he is grey,
   For a young man's heart is full of love,
   Go away, old man, go away.

3. Put your two cigarettes in
   And let me hear you cough, sir.
   (hack, hack)
   Very good indeed, sir,
   Tell me what you need sir,
   One two, three, four, five ...

4. Ittulaiti tulaiti
   Aippatalinlangutok
   Samueli Samueli Samuelimik
   Tupake tupakilo pevarimi
   Te-da-lum-de, te-da-lum-de.

5. Cards and dice
   Are the devil's device;
   God's desire
   Is to put them in the fire.

6. Tobacco is a filthy weed,
    I likes it!
    It satisfies no normal need,
    I likes it!
    It makes you thin, it makes you lean,
    It takes the hair right off your bean,
    It's the worst damn stuff I've ever seen—
    I likes it!

7. Coomb sat on the powder keg,
    Singing soft and low,
    Smoking on his cigarette,
    But Coomb he didn't know.
    He began to whoop and cough
    And boom the powder it went off
    And Coomb had found some other place to go.

8. The non-starter
    Is smarter.

9. Rum is two dollars a gallon,
    And whiskey two or three,
    And if you wants your baccy
    You lay out your sixty-three.

10. Ittle ottle, blue bottle,
    Ittle ottle oo,
    If your father chews tobacco
    Out goes you.

11. Tobacco is a dirty weed,
    Because the devil sowed the seed,
    It rents your pockets, dirts your clothes,
    And makes a chimney of your nose.

12. Even pinky now is high-brow
    For a fellow with the shakes,
    As he pays an extra quarter
    For the juice from a pound of grapes.

13. Clouds break
    Sun shine,
    Less ice,
    More wine.

14. In heaven we have no rum
    So here we have a great sum.

15. When Tom Murdoch is dead and in his grave,
    For Bavarian Beer he will not crave,
    For on his tombstone will be wrote
    Many a gallon flowed down his throat.

16. 'Twas you who made me wear old clothes,
    'Twas you who made me friends me foes,
    But since you are so near me nose,
    Tip her up and down she goes.

17. When the rum's in the keg,
    The tongue don't wag.

18. The juice of the apple makes cider so fine,
    The juice of the grape makes red and white wine.

19. Here's to prohibition,
    The devil take it!
    They've stolen our wine,
    So now we make it.

20. In Greedy Harbour I went one time,
    I picked up a jar, I thought 'twas wine,
    I picked it up, I thought it was wine
    I guzzled it down, 'twas turkentine.

21. Oh whiskey, you're the devil,
    You are leading me astray,
    Oh why to the lock-up
    You are bringing me today,
    You humbled me and tumbled me,
    And robbed me of good clothes,
    Oh whiskey, you have given me
    Red blossoms on my nose.

22. Said Aristotle unto Plato,
    "Have another baked potato?"
    Said Plato unto Aristotle,
    "Thank you, I prefer the bottle."

23. And now we're in the bonny place,
    The island of St. Pierre,
    Rum is gone up, boys,
    Since the last time we were here.

24. Daddy's getting big and fat,
    The rest of us are thinner,
    'Cause the nickels go for beer
    To wash down Daddy's dinner.

25. There's the love of a maid and the love of a man,
    And the love of a baby that's unafraid,
    All living since time began
    But the best love, the love of all loves,
    Even greater than the love for Mother,
    Is the greatest, greatest, greatest love,
    Of one dead drunk for another.

26. Our fathers, who were very wise,
    Would wash their throats before their eyes.

27. Before the Travellers' Joy you pass,
    Stop in and have a parting glass.
    Now that your journey's almost over
    Stop in, your spirits to recover.

28. I've trusted often to my sorrow—
    Pay today and trust tomorrow.

29. Here's to the land of the shamrocks so green,
    Here's to each boy and his darling colleen,
    Here's to the one we love dearest and most,
    May God speed old Ireland, that's an Irishman's toast.

30. Madam, have you any good wine,
    Parlez-vous?
    Madam, have you any good wine,
    Parlez-vous?
    Madam, have you any good wine,
    Fit for a soldier of the line,
    With a hinky-dinky parlez-vous.

31. If at a party I should be
    With ladies of a high degree,
    Myself to custom would conform
    And stay at night 'til three next morn.

32. Starkle, starkle, little twink
    Who the heck I are you think,
    I'm not under what you call,
    The affluence of incohol,
    I feel so foolish, I don't know who's me
    The drunker I sit here the longer I be.

33. Here's to ourselves
    And hold your luff,
    Plenty of prizes
    And plenty of duff.

• • •

3. "Put your two cigarettes in …" is a counting-out game. Each child holds out two index fingers, and pretends to cough. A number is given, and the leader counts around and the finger she lands on is folded down until all but one is out. I was taught this game by Mary Niamh McGettigan of Harbour Main.

4. "Ittulaiti tulaiti" is an Inuktitut song, known in a number of versions, that loosely translates as "My dear lovely old man, / I am tired of waiting to wed thee / Sam, Sam, Sam, / Because he has lots of / Beaver tabaccy." This version is as sung by Margaret Suksagiak, recorded in Tim Borlase's *Songs of Labrador*. The refrain is probably "Diddle-um-dee."

5. From *Random Passage* by Bernice Morgan.

6. From *Legacy of Laughter* by Jack Fitzgerald.

8. From anti-smoking ads, put out by the Tuberculosis Association.

9. From *A History of Little Bay East, Fortune Bay* by Clyde Scott.

12. From the *Dictionary of Newfoundland English*. Pinky is very cheap sherry or port.

13. From *Harbour Grace Standard*, 1883.

14. From a fridge magnet I saw in the Downhome shop.

15. From Fred Adams, and also quoted in Jack Fitzgerald's *Newfoundland Fireside Stories*.

16. A toast recorded by Cecil H. Parsons in *Effie's Angels*.

18. Recorded by R.F. Sparkes in *The Winds Softly Sigh*, but most likely learned from the *Royal Readers*.

19. I believe I read this in an issue of *Saltscapes*.

20. From Greenleaf and Mansfield's *Ballads and Sea Songs of Newfoundland*. Greedy Harbour is Grady Harbour in Labrador.

21. From *Legacy of Laughter* by Jack Fitzgerald.

22. From *Legacy of Laughter* by Jack Fitzgerald.

23. From *A History of Little Bay East, Fortune Bay* by Clyde Scott.

24. "Daddy's Getting Big and Fat" is a children's skipping rhyme.

25. I saw this in a literacy book at the North West River library but haven't been able to locate it again.

26. To "wash your throat before your eyes" is to have a drink of rum first thing in the morning. From Les Harris in *Growing Up with Verse*.

27. The first half of the Travellers' Joy verse was on the town side of the tavern sign, and the second half on the country side. The Travellers' Joy was in the west end of St. John's.

28. "I've trusted often" was in a tavern on Water Street. From Michael P. Murphy, *Pathways through Yesterday*.

30. From George England's *Vikings of the Age*, 1924.

32. "Starkle, Starkle" is a variation, with Newfoundland linguistic constructions, of a well-known verse, sometimes attributed to Charlie Drake, that ends, "So one more drink to fill up my cup / I got all sober to Sunday up."

33. This is Long John Silver's toast, quoted in Jack Fitzgerald's *Treasure Island Revisited*. My father was more likely to quote from one of his own verses: "And so I say, with care unvexed, / 'To Hell with Winter, Spring will come,' / and act on Long John Silver's text, / 'Darby McGrath; Fetch aft the rum!'"

Sing Holly, Sing Ivy!

29. The Christmas Season

My father, who escaped being born a Victorian by a matter of months, used to recall for us "going out with the wren boys" at Christmas time, collecting pennies with a dead bird on a stick on St. Stephen's Day. He taught us the little song he and his friends sang to coax the coppers out of jaded housewives and hung-over revellers, and I felt a real thrill of recognition when I heard it years later coming out of the mouths of a famous folk group from the U.S. What a revelation to discover we were the "folk," just as quaint and authentic as Woody Guthrie or Leadbelly. Who'd have guessed it?

There wasn't much that thrilled me about Christmas. I liked the crèche, but the anticipation of presents was always too painful and disappointing in a family the size of ours. Christmas always seemed to involve washing mountains of dishes and being on best behaviour for far too long. The dog usually threatened to die from eating tinsel or chocolate or something, my cousins always got better presents than I did, and the agony of writing the obligatory thank-you note to my aunt in Montreal put a pall on everything.

St. Stephen's Day, as my father knew it, would have been welcome, but the day of the wren boys was long gone by the time I arrived, and it probably wouldn't have been extended to girls anyway. My Boxing Day involved Father getting togged out in a top hat and morning coat, to make the rounds of the Archbishop's Palace and Government House, while we sat home with our mother and received a slow parade of similarly dressed and increasingly inebriated doctors and lawyers. It was always an extremely pleasant day, and, if a child was quick with a drink or a coat, there was often a silver coin slipped into your hand by way of reward.

One Christmas custom I came to dread was the practice of admiring the tree. Groups of children would come to the front door, knocking formally, and ask to see the tree. You had to let them in, plug in the tree lights (which were never left on unattended), and then maybe your mother would offer them a chocolate or an apple. I always felt that our tree, our presents, our household were under intense scrutiny and that we were failing some critical test.

Admiring the tree usually happened after Boxing Day, but one year a gaggle of youngsters turned up on Christmas afternoon, right after dinner. Our mother indicated that they were to be invited in, and, when they shuffled in through the porch, I saw that some had no boots over their shoes, others had no shoes under their boots, and there was hardly a pair of socks between the lot of them. After the mandatory gawp at the tree, my older sisters were told to take them into the kitchen and feed them our leftovers, obviously the only dinner they were going to get that day. Even then, I knew my mother's grim anger was at their poverty, not at the children themselves.

I can't imagine the courage it took those kids to climb up from the Cribbies, through Rabbittown, where they might have been recognized, to forage for a meal among the comfortable middle-class houses of St. John's. But after that, Christmas seemed a sham and I definitely didn't believe in Santa Claus any longer. However, there were still the Christmas songs and verses to enjoy, and they make quite an innocent contrast with the ones I collected from children today.

> 1. Jingle bells, Batman smells,
> Robin got a gun,
> Shot a plane and went insane
> In nineteen eighty-one,
> Dashing through the snow
> On a broken pair of skis
> Over the hills we go
> Smashing through the trees (ha, ha, ha).
> The snow is turning red
> I think I'm almost dead,
> Someone took a .44
> And shot me through the head.

2. Our bones are old,
   We're very cold,
   We shiver, shiver,
   Shake with cold.

3. See, my stocking's much too small,
   It won't hold anything at all,
   Guess I'll go and borrow Ma's—
   Won't that surprise old Santa Claus.

4. Old Santa Claus travels about doing good,
   A wonderful mission is his,
   So children be good to that wonderful friend
   When you find out who the little man is.

5. Christians awake! Salute the happy morn
   Wherein the Saviour of the World was born.

6. My father stole the parson's sheep
   And Merry Christmas we will keep,
   And not say aught about it.

7. Our neighbour here is a worthy man
   And to his house we have brought our wren,
   Sing holly, sing ivy, sing ivy, sing holly,
   He'll give us a drop to drown melancholy.

8. The wren, the wren, the king of all birds,
   St. Stephen's Day was caught in the firs,
   Although he is little his honour is great,
   So stand up kind lady and give us a treat.
   A barrel full of money
   A belly full of beer,
   We wish you a Merry Christmas
   And a Happy New Year.

9. Oidhche chullainn Challuinn chruaidh
   Thàninig mise le m'dhuan gu taig.
   Thubhairt am bodach rium le gruaim
   Buailidh mi do chluais le preas.
   Labhair á chailleach a b'fhearr na'n t-òr
   Gum bu chòir mo leigeil a staigh
   Aui son na dh'ithinn-sa de bhiadh
   Agus deuran beag sìos leis.

   Fógramuid an Ghorta,
   Amach go tír na d-Turchach;
   Ó nocht go bliadhain ó nocht,
   Agus o nocht féin amch.

10. Earthgamer, Girthgamer
    Augish, playing dish,
    Drive out the hunger,
    Bring in the grub.
    From this day forward
    To the end of the year.

11. Up with the bottle and down with the pan,
    A penny or twopence to bury the wren.

12. Here I stand upon the stage,
    And quite a little figure,
    If the girls don't like me now,
    They'll like me when I'm bigger.

13. Here I stand upon the stage,
    I never stood up here before,
    And by the scary way it feels
    I'll never do it any more.

14. Now may this bless your hearth and fold,
    Shut out the wolf and keep out the cold,
    Take care of your fire and be of good cheer,
    May peace and joy be with you throughout the new year.

15. 'Tis just a wreath of mistletoe
    We send to you today,
    In token of our deepest love
    For you so far away.

16. Oh dear, oh dear, I feel so queer,
    My heart goes pitta pat,
    So I think I'll make a bow
    And leave you after that.

17. While shepherds wash their socks by night
    All seated round the tub,
    The angel of the Lord came down
    And they began to scrub.

18. Nine-one-one, nine-one-one,
    Santa Claus is dead,
    Rudolph took a .44
    And shot him through the head.
    Oh Barbie doll, Barbie doll,
    Tried to save his life,
    Teddy bear came to life
    And stabbed him with a knife.

• • •

1. Collected from children in Cartwright, Labrador, in 2006.

2. "Our Bones Are Old" is a Christmas recitation from St. Mary's Bay, collected from Joseph Dobbin by Alice Lannon and Michael McCarthy.

3. From Musgrave Harbour, recorded in "Folklore, the School and the Child," by Sheila Maud Saunders, 1982.

4. "Old Santa Claus" is a verse from Labrador, where, thanks to the Grenfell Mission, Santa has a much longer history than he does in Newfoundland. Recorded by Margaret Davis of Cartwright in *Them Days*.

5. From Marion Saunders Tharp, recorded in *Them Days*.

6. From Arthur Rich of Rocky Cove, Labrador, published in *Them Days*.

7. By W.P., from *Christmas Bells*, 1893.

8. From my father, J.M.F. McGrath.

9. Allan MacArthur recalls reciting "Oidhche chullainn" at every house he visited at New Year's. The Gaelic translates as "On a cold, frosty night of New Year's Eve, / I came with my rhyme to a house, / The old man said to me with a frown / I'll hit you on the ear with a briar. / Said the old woman who was better than gold / That I should let you in / For all the little food that I would eat / And a little drink to go with it." This was recorded by Margaret Bennett in *The Last Stronghold*.

10. Frank Furlong recalls reciting "Earthgamer, Girthgamer" on New Year's day while bouncing a loaf of bread off the door of their house in St. John's. Philip Hiscock has identified it as a variant of the Irish New Year's rhyme: "Fórgramud an Ghorta, / Amach go tír na d-Turchach; / O nocht go bliadhain ó nocht, / Agus o nocht fein amch. We warn famine / To retire to the country of the Turks / From this night to this night / Twelvemonth, / And even this very night." Quoted by Philip Hiscock in *The Newfoundland Quarterly*.

12. This is probably the best known of the school or Christmas recitations, the first one a child usually learned. The "stage" is sometimes a chair.

13. Collected from my neighbour, Margaret Hammond, Beachy Cove, Conception Bay.

14. "Now may this bless your hearth and fold" is the old Mummers blessing, given with a lighted candle.

15. From Otto Tucker's *That Nothing Be Lost*.

16. A Christmas recitation from St. Mary's Bay, collected from Joseph Dobbin by Alice Lannon and Michael McCarthy.

17. From Gary Saunders's *Free Wind Home*.

18. From Hillary Learning, Cartwright, Labrador, 2006.

Ambrose Shea Skedaddled Away

30. Political Verses

It has often been said that the favourite amusement of all Newfoundlanders is politics. This is evident in the political slogans and rhymes that have emerged from time to time to encourage, castigate, and mock politicians. Election verses were popular in Newfoundland during the election of 1836, and probably earlier, and are still being appropriated today to mock or support candidates for political office.

Politics has never had much attraction for me, probably because I saw it all too personally. My great-grandfather stood for Placentia-St. Mary's, and was elected, as were my grandfather and my great-uncle. I was seven years old when my father fought his first political campaign. He had the unusual experience of being named to cabinet as Minister of Health before he actually ran for office, and, while I do remember waking up to see his picture on the front page of the newspaper, he still went to the same office to work (he had been Assistant Deputy Minister) and nothing else seemed very different. I have no recollection of that first election at all, although I remember the subsequent ones.

My most vivid election memory is of delivering pamphlets in the district of St. Mary's and having doors slammed in my face and insults hurled after my hastily retreating figure. It did not happen very often as my father was a popular figure—possibly because as a general practitioner he had suffered through the depression with the voters—and he won every election he fought by a very wide margin. My problem was that I could not understand why he did not win 100 percent of the votes. Every vote against him was, for me, a personal and humiliating defeat.

One of the most vivid recollections I have of my father's political career was watching him perform at a public meeting in Branch, where he was loudly and unremittingly heckled by a well-to-do widow who had only recently come back from the States. Although Branch was not one of my father's strongholds, the more she interrupted, the more the audience turned against her until a carefully timed rejoinder about her new fur coat evoked a roar of laughter from the audience and she beat a hasty retreat.

On the way home, my father gave me some advice should I ever decide to throw my hat into the ring: run every election as if you are going to lose it, and develop a thick skin. It was only when I was older that I realized that, unlike my father, most politicians are so remarkably touchy that a slogan like "Clyde lied!" or "Hit the road, Jack" really gets to them.

1. Carson, Morris and Kent forever
   The sacred cause they will promote
   The chains of slavery they will sever
   In spite of the apostate's brazen throat.

2. Oh, did you see Dr. Kielly O,
   His boots all polished so highly O,
   With his three cocked hats
   And his double knot bow
   And his riddle to coax the ladies O.

3. Oh yellow, yellow Douglas,
   Oh yellow, yellow man,
   Here is a yellow doughboy,
   Come eat it if you can.

4. Ambrose Shea
   Skedaddled away
   To paddle his own canoe.

5. Morine, Mott and Winter, three haters of gin,
   Went forth for to capture the votes of Burin,
   Said Winter to Mott, as St. Peter's is handy,
   You might nip across for a drop of good brandy.
   I'm persuaded such seasoned old voters as these
   The gentle persuasion of Temp'rance won't please.
   To win the political battle I've come,
   And to win it, I'm certain, there's nothing like rum.

6. Oh 'tis oh me Johnnie Poker,
   Sure Ned Morris is a joker,
   And Tom Murphy is a soaker, oh,
   Ned Jackman is a jader,
   And John Scott is a trader,
   Oh this fall they'll have to go, go, go!

7. Vote for Julia
   She won't fool ya.

8. Diefenbaker,
   Thief and faker.

9. We'll finish the drive
   In sixty-five.
   (Thanks to Mr. Pearson.)

10. Joey, the name high over all,
    In heaven and earth and sky,
    Angels and men before him fall,
    And devils before him fly.

11. Vote for Wyatt
    She won't be quiet.

12. Clyde
    Lied!

13. The last living father is dead
    The last living father is dead,
    Oh take off his glasses
    And put him to bed,
    The last living father is dead.

14. Gather the "H"s while you may,
    H-old time is still h-flying,
    The h-eye that's h-eying you 'ere today
    Tomorrow will be 'ie-ing.

15. Remember the day
    When Carter and Shea
    Went over the way
    To barter away
    The rights of Terra Nova.

16. The light on Pond Rock
    And the Marconi pole
    Put in John Scammell
    And turned out Monroe.

17. Ollie Vardy
     A master cook,
     Sometimes doubles
     As a master crook.

18. The prophet, George Gushue, man,
     Oh, 'tis now he cuts a dash,
     By dad, he's like a boo-man,
     Since he cut off his mustache.

19. The PCs came down like the Feds on the cod,
     And no one could tally their numbers but God;
     The numerous votes were like trout on the ponds,
     Where the cool waters flow to quench all of St. John's.

20. Don't vote for she;
     She's not for he.

21. Life is good, life is earnest
     And the grave is not the goal,
     Dust thou are and dust returneth
     Has been said of Cashin's coal.

22. Vote, vote, vote for dear old Brian,   23. Lie,
     Who's that knocking on the door?   Deny,
     If it's Michael let him in   Then act
     And we'll have a drop of gin,   Surprised.
     And we won't vote for Brian any more.

24. Sir Richard Squires, he promised a lot,
     When he first got elected,
     But what he did for us poor folk
     Was not what we expected.

25. She took a lickin'
     But kept on tickin'.

26. I like a pension … in committee,
    But my agreement, more's the pity,
    Must be made public, and of course
    This will not do, because the force
    Of the opinion of my friends
    Might be that I served private ends.
    What shall I do? Well, there's a way
    To get both credit and the pay.
    So, in committee, I'll agree
    But when the whole wide world can see
    I'll vote it down. By this invention
    I'll get both credit and the pension.

27. Big Jim from Oderin the Bait Act Commander,
    You'd thought you'd got over the men from Burgeo,
    But they haven't forgot all the fine things you promised,
    At the general election just four years ago.

28. Bond's too green to burn,
    There's no doubt about that,
    Whilst a shoehorn he'll turn
    For to get on his hat.

29. A young fisherman from La Scie
    Who bided on bare bread and tea
    Said the League's politics
    Are just richbelly tricks—
    That won't get a rise out of me.

30. A weapon that comes down as still
    As snowflakes fall upon the sod,
    But executes a freeman's will;
    And from it force nor doors nor locks
    Can bar you—'Tis the Ballot Box.

31. There's Charles Fox Bennett, *alanna*,
    He's brought out an elegant boat,
    To cruise round the island, dear Mickey,
    To try to secure every vote.

32. When in doubt,
    Stamp and shout,
    Wave your arms
    And run about.

33. Are you lonely, Neddie,
    For the life that once you had,
    Walking on the beach rocks
    And fishing with your dad?
    Are you ever angry
    That they led you to believe
    There'd be work right here for all of you,
    No one would have to leave?

34. There was a little fan
    And he joined a little clan,
    Masked from his neck to his forehead;
    When he was known he was very, very good,
    But when he was masked he was horrid.

35. Dimple, dimple, Happy John,
    You can really turn 'em on,
    With your wavy hair and dimple,
    You can charm both sash and wimple.

36. Liberal, Tory,
    Same old story.

1. The "Carson, Morris and Kent" verse was popular during the election of 1836.

2. Dr. Edward Kielly, founder of the Native's Society, was the professional rival of Carson and in 1838 he was imprisoned for calling John Kent a liar.

3. In 1848, the "Injun meal and Molasses Year" when corn meal was given to the poor, a Mr. Douglas was charged with issuing relief.

4. When Ambrose Shea was appointed governor in 1886, the announcement caused such public protest that his name was withdrawn and he accepted a position in the Bahamas, from whence he retired to England.

5. A by-election in 1892, when "a river of rum flowed from the Conservative side," produced the ditty about Morine, Mott, and Winter.

6. A parody of the traditional hauling shanty "Johnny Poker" was titled "Haul on the Plunder" when it was composed during the election of 1904.

7. When Julia Salter Earle ran for a position on city council in 1923, she urged citizens to vote for her with this verse.

8. In 1962, when John Diefenbaker tried to end the special subsidy Newfoundland received under Confederation's Term 29, the battle cry was "Diefenbaker, thief and faker."

9. "We'll Finish the Drive" was on a billboard acknowledging the Liberal government subsidy for paving the section of the Trans Canada Highway between St. John's and Port aux Basques.

10. "Joey the Name" is a play on a traditional hymn, originally invoking the name of Jesus and often used for protection against ghosts and demons, now invoking Smallwood.

11. Dorothy Wyatt was the first woman elected to city council, and the first councillor to be elected after she was dead, which will be a hard

record to beat. In 1973, she turned insult to good advantage with her campaign slogan.

12. Premier Clyde Wells rolled back the contracts for civil servants in 1991 only to be greeted with buttons, placards, and shouts that proclaimed "Clyde lied."

13. J.R. Smallwood often referred to himself as "the last living father of Confederation." Journalist Kathryn Welbourn penned this obituary for him.

14. "Gather the 'H's" is a parody of the old English verse "Gather Ye Rosebuds," making fun of a political hopeful with an accent similar to that of John Efford.

15. "Remember the Day" is a reference to the second last attempt to bring Newfoundland and Labrador into Confederation.

16. The lighthouse at Pond Rock was an election issue in 1928 when Walter Monroe lost Bonavista Centre.

17. Oliver Vardy was at various times a radio announcer, a M.H.A., director of tourism development, and editor of the *Fisherman Workers Tribune*. He served prison time for armed robbery early in his life, and, when later charged with fraud, bribery, and breach of trust, he fled to Panama, where he escaped extradition to Canada, and then went to Florida, where he fought extradition until his death. The rhyme was made up by Terry Carter.

18. "George Gushue's Mustache" is from the *Daily News*, 1903.

19. "The PCs came down like the Feds on the cod" was written by Ed Smith.

20. "Don't Vote for She" was written about a candidate in the 1972 provincial election, and recorded by Herbert Pottle in *Dawn without Light*, but nobody seems to recall who the candidate was, even by a process of elimination.

21. "Life is Good," a parody of Longfellow's "Psalm of Life," was aimed at Major Peter Cashin, who was arguing in the House about doing some-

thing for the fishery and less for the railway. The Cashins had a fuel business. The last line was originally "Was not spoken of the soul."

22. "Vote, Vote, Vote" is a children's song that acknowledges the adult practice of buying votes with liquor. It is sung to the tune of "Tramp, Tramp, Tramp, the Boys are Marching."

23. "Lie, deny, then act surprised" was said to be advice to the new politician.

24. Squires was the Prime Minister of Newfoundland from 1919 to 1923 and 1928 to 1932. He was accused of falsifying minutes of Cabinet to cover up fees he had paid to himself out of the public purse, prompting 10,000 rioters to attack the Colonial Building.

25. According to Ray Guy, it was women's activist Dorothy Inglis who "took a lickin.'"

26. "I like a pension" was my father J.M.F. McGrath's response when Jim Greene agreed to Members' pensions in Committee but attacked it in the House.

27. The subject of this verse, my grandfather James Fanning McGrath, was running in the 1893 election. This rhyme was often sung to the tune of "The Ryans and The Pittmans," in which he also makes an appearance.

28. Sir Robert Bond was Prime Minister from 1900 to 1909.

29. "The League" was the League for Responsible Government.

30. "The Ballot Box" was quoted by Robert Bond in his farewell speech in 1914.

31. The *alanna* and Mickey addressed in "There's Charles Fox Bennett" were Irish voters. *Alanna* means dear one.

32. "When in Doubt" is another of Ray Guy's many contributions to political commentary in Newfoundland and Labrador.

33. From *A Fit Month for Dying* by M.T. Dohaney.

34. This verse, from the Mercy College magazine *Inter Nos* in the early 1930s, suggests that Newfoundlanders were following what was happening in America with the Ku Klux Klan. It is a parody of "There was a little girl / And she had a little curl, / Right in the middle of her forehead, / And when she was good she was very, very good, / But when she was bad she was horrid."

35. Quoted by John C. Crosbie in his introduction to Ray Guy's book *Ray Guy: The Smallwood Years*. Guy had identified Crosbie as the sex-appeal candidate at the Liberal leadership convention. I suppose it's possible Crosbie didn't know exactly how ironic Guy was being.

36. "Liberal, Tory, / Same old story" was an NDP slogan.

Mackerel Skies and Mares' Tails

31. The Weather

An old Newfoundland joke is "If you don't like the weather, wait a minute." That was just one of many weather epithets I grew up with. Others included, "Everyone complains about the weather but nobody ever does anything about it," my mother's injunction to "Pay no attention to the weather; just makes your plans and proceed," and my own favourite, "There's no such thing as bad weather, just bad outfitting."

None of these observations apply to Labrador, of course, for in Labrador the weather is infinitely better than in Newfoundland. The winters are sunny, the summers are warm and dry, the weather can be consistent for days or weeks at a time, and the Labradorians try to keep it a secret so as not to have to share it with anyone else. True, it can be a bit chilly in January, but compared to the icy slush and horizontal rains of the Avalon, it merely induces a pleasant *frisson*.

Predicting the weather is as old as weather itself. I was startled, while idly perusing the Bible one day, to come across Matthew 16, verses 2 and 3: "When it is evening, it will be fair weather, for the sky is red, and in the morning it will be foul weather today, for the sky is red and lowering." I wonder if it says anywhere in the Bible that if Nan's corns ache, or if you can smell the outhouse from the kitchen, or if the soot falls in the chimney, it will rain, and if the children or the goats are galing, it will be stormy?

We even project our weather predictions backward onto people. Not long ago, I overheard a man describe how he was changing planes in Toronto when he suddenly saw his ex-wife bearing down on him. "Her face was on 29," he said, a reference to the barometer predicting stormy weather.

Nowadays, we count on satellite photos to tell us what the weather will be, and, if they are wrong, the worst that is likely to happen is a sudden soaking or a sunburn. However, there was a time when reading the weather was a matter of life and death for the men and women of Newfoundland and Labrador. If gales blew, boats sank, and, if fish got fousty, families starved. That was the harsh reality behind the weather verses I collected, some of which I include here.

1. Red sky at night,
Sailors' delight;
Red sky at morning,
Sailors take warning.

2. If you don't want your pork to ruin,
Kill your pigs at the full of the moon.

3. A Saturday's moon,
Comes all too soon.

4. Clear moon,
Frost soon.

5. St. Swithen's Day
If we have rain,
Forty days
It will remain.

6. Bright northern lights above the hill
A fine day, then a storm foretell.

7. The sun drawing water
Bide home with wife and daughter.

8. Pale moon doth rain,
Red moon doth blow,
White moon do neither
Rain nor snow.

9. Rain before seven,
Done before eleven.

10. Brass monkeys beware …
'Tis that time of year.

11. Here I come, bold Hercules,
    I've come to stem the weather,
    I'll take the rainbow from the sky
    And tie both ends together.

12. If February gives much snow,
    A fine summer it doth foreshow.

13. April showers
    Bring May flowers,
    But it also wrinkles.
    Grey flannel trousers.

14. The West wind always brings wet weather
    The East wind, wet and cold together,
    The South wind surely brings us rain,
    The North wind blows it back again.

15. If Candlemas Day comes in clear and fine,
    The worst of the winter is left behind,
    If Candlemas Day comes in foul and glum,
    The worst of the winter is yet to come.

16. If the wind's in the east on Candlemas Day
    There it will stick 'til the end of May.

17. If the crows fly low,
    We'll have plenty of snow.

18. Seabirds keeping near the land
    Tell a storm is near at hand,
    But flying seaward out of sight,
    You may stay and fish all night.

19. January tests,
    February tries,
    'Tis March decides
    If ye lives or dies.

20. Evening grey, morning red,
    Sets a traveller in his bed;
    Evening red, morning grey,
    Sets a traveller on his way.

21. When the corn is in the shock,
    Then the fish is to the rocks.

22. Mackerel skies
    And mares' tails
    Cause lofty ships
    To carry low sails.

23. Mackerel sky, mackerel sky,
    Not long wet and not long dry.

24. If the goats come home in files,
    Get your fish in covered piles.

25. The old moon in the arms of the new
    Bodes no good for me nor you.

26. When the rain comes before the wind,
    Halyards, sheets and reef-points mind.

27. When your nose is itching on top,
    That's a sign of wind and lop;
    When your nose is itching in under,
    That's the sign of rain and thunder.

28. Mackerel skies bring showers
    Inside forty-eight hours.

29. When the snipe bawls,
    The lobster crawls.

30. As the day lengthens,
    So the cold strengthens.

31. When the wind veers against the sun,
    Trust it not, for back 'twill run.

32. If the first days in April be foggy,
    Rain in June will make the grass boggy.

33. A dripping June
    Brings all things in tune.

34. If St. Vitus Day is rainy weather,
    It will rain for thirty days together.

35. When the winds of October
    Won't make the leaves go,
    There'll be a frosty winter
    With banks of snow.

36. If ducks do slide at Hollantide,
    At Christmas they will swim.

37. Easterly winds the glitter brings,
    And silver trees and other things.

38. If St. Matthew's Day is bright and clear,
    It means good weather for the coming year.

39. If life were all fair weather,
    As the fleeting days go by,
    We would never know the beauty
    Of the rainbow in the sky.

• • •

1. This is our modern version of the Biblical passage from the Book of Matthew.

2-5. From *Devine's Folk Lore*.

7-9. From *Downhome* (November 2004).

10. By K.T., the *Telegram* cartoonist, December 8, 2004.

11. "Bold Hercules" sounds like something from the Mummers play.

12. From Lannon and McCarthy, *Fables, Fairies and Folklore of Newfoundland*.

13. From *Legacy of Laughter* by Jack Fitzgerald.

14. This verse is actually about the Plymouth climate, not Newfoundland's. I don't know how relevant it would be on the west side of the Atlantic.

15. From Len Margaret's *Fish and Brewis, Toutens and Tales*. Candelmas Day, February 2, is the feast of the Purefication of the Virgin Mary, when candles are blessed.

18. From the *Twillingate Times*, by W.I. Jesperson.

19. From Ron Pumphrey's *Human Beans*.

24. From the *Dictionary of Newfoundland English*.

27. From Les Harris, *Growing Up with Verse*.

29. The snipe bawls after sunset.

34. From Lannon and McCarthy. St. Vitus Day is June 15.

36. From Lannon and McCarthy. Hollantide is November 11.

37. Glitter is also called silver thaw in Newfoundland. From W. Swansborough, *Newfoundland Months*.

38. From Lannon and McCarthy. St. Matthew's Day is September 21.

Ashes to Ashes

32. Epitaphs and Memorials

The last word about a person is usually written on his or her grave-stone. I grew up across from Belvedere Cemetery, and it was not unusual for adults to wander between the graves as if it were a park, and children were allowed to explore and linger over the tombstones as long as they were respectful of the dead. I liked the lambs and the held hands, the roses and the Celtic crosses, and I loved the small waves of melancholy the epitaphs induced, especially those of the babies. It all seemed so utterly romantic and sad.

The epitaphs at Belvedere were generally solemn and pious: name, dates, and maybe a verse of the Bible or some other spiritual saying. I don't recall ever having seen any of the numerous humorous or witty epitaphs that I heard or read about. Things have changed in the last fifty years—nowadays, anything goes. A widower of my acquaintance, one of the most genuinely spiritual men I know, recently had "I did it my way!" inscribed on the stone over his wife's grave. "It's what she wanted," he said, with a shrug. Perhaps his acceptance of her wishes was why theirs was such a long and successful marriage.

If anyone had ever asked me—and thank goodness they didn't—I was going to suggest that the epitaph on my mother's grave should read "Often difficult but never boring." As I got older, I realized that was probably the best I could ever hope to have for my own stone, and it was then I decided I'd be cremated and put in the compost bin.

Most of these epitaphs which follow are said to be real but I cannot confirm the existence of any of them. However, given that many of them were located in isolated outports where people had to fadge for themselves without the assistance of funeral directors and stone engravers, it is quite possible that local humorists took advantage of their literacy to compose these memorials for the unsuspecting mourners. It is also possible that those who took up residence below these stones didn't mind in the least that their last words drew a smile.

1. Ashes to ashes,
   Dust to dust,
   The lord won't have he
   So the devil must.

2. Death rides on every breeze
   He lurks in every flower,
   Each season has its own disease
   Its perils every hour.

3. 'Twas three days out from Newfoundland
   When overboard he falled,
   And as he was agoin' down
   Upon the Lord he called.

4. Here lies the body of W.W.
   Never more will he trouble you, trouble you.
   His fat bank book he often used,
   And the big doughboy he never refused.
   Fish and brewis he liked the best,
   And the big bangbelly. Let the poor man rest.

5. Here lies the body of John Power
   Who played with the gun at Cabot Tower,
   The gun went off and shook the nation
   And they found John Power at the Railway Station.

6. As I am now, so must you be,
   Therefore prepare to follow me,
   As you are now so once was I,
   Therefore prepare yourself to die.

7. Don't attempt to climb a tree,
   For that's what caused the death of me.

8. Here lies the body of Solomon Dawe
   The finest man you ever saw,
   Also his daughter Mary Ann,
   Who was killed by a fall from a catamaran.

9. Man's strong desire for life we daily see,
   And few who view this place would change with me,
   Yet, serious reader, tell which is best
   The tiresome journey or the traveller's rest.

10. Here lies the body of Mary Jane,
    Josiah was her husband's name
    She caught a cold in a shower of rain,
    And that was how she heaven did gain,
    She suffered much for a very long while,
    And is not buried here, but in the Straits of Belle Isle.

11. Here lies I and my two daughters,
    Kilt by drinking old bog waters.
    If we had stuck to Epsom salts,
    We shouldn't be lying in these here vaults.

12. In love I lived, in grief I died,
    I asked for rum, but was denied.

13. Here lies Michael Ollerhead,
    He died from cold caught in his head.
    It brought on fever and rhumatiz,
    Which ended me—for here I is!

14. Here lies the man Richard, and Mary his wife,
    Whose surname was Prichard, they lived without strife,
    And the reason was plain, they abounded in riches,
    They had no care or pain, and his wife wore the britches.

15. Here lies the body of Mary Ann Ford,
    We hope her soul has gone to the Lord,
    But if for hell she had changed this life,
    She'd be better off there than as John Ford's wife.

16. Ye little ducks lift up your head,
    Your enemy is lying dead,
    No more he'll point his great long gun,
    No more he'll make you poor ducks run.

17. Beneath this clay lies Paddy Day,
    The bailiff and the bum!
    When he died the devil cried,
    "Come with me, Paddy, come!"

18. An excellent husband was this Mr. Danner,
    He lived in a thoroughly decent manner,
    He may have had troubles
    But they burst like bubbles
    He's now at peace with Jane, Mary, Susan and Hannah.

19. Here lies the body of John Dawley and Molly,
    They're not dead, just sleeping here,
    Rise again in the fall of the year,
    And ship the fish at Carbonear.

20. Here lies John and Rich and Ben,
    Three lawyers and three honest men—
    God works miracles now and then.

21. One army of the living God
    To his command we bow,
    Part of the host have crossed the flood
    And part are crossing now.

22. To this give heed, ye passers by,
    Thus as you are, so once was I,
    And that like me you soon must be
    Then oh, prepare to follow me.

23. Affliction sore long time I bore,
    Physician's art was vain,
    'Til Death did ease and God did please
    To cure me of my pain.

24. And now his long life's voyage o'er
    And past the perils of the sea,
    Receive him on the blissful shore
    To everlasting rest with thee.

25. My anvil and my hammer are declining,
    My bellows, too, has lost its wind,
    My fire extinct, my forge decayed,
    And in the dust my voice is laid,
    My coal is spent, my iron is gone,
    My last nail driven, and my work done.

26. Here lies the body of Tiny Tim,
    In life we didn't see much of him.

27. Just a little cradle,
    Just a little child,
    Just a few short fleeting years
    And then a girl so wild.
    Soon she reaches womanhood,
    Then comes on old age,
    And this completes the journey
    From the cradle to the grave.

28. Don't weep for me now,
    Weep for me never,
    'Cause I'm gonna do nuttin'
    Forever and ever.

29. Here lies the body of Nora Moore,
    She had husbands by the score,
    If she had lived a few years more
    There'd be nar man left on the Southern Shore.

30. Here lies the body of William Drake,
    Oh pray for his poor soul's sake.
    He had a wife always growlin' and scoffin',
    So he sought repose in a twelve-dollar coffin.

31. Weep not for us, our friends so dear,
    We are not dead but sleepeth,
    We are not yours but Christ's alone,
    He loved us best and took us home.

32. If you should see a white horse go by,
    Then you will be the next to die.
    They wrap you up in a big white sheet
    And throw you down about six feet deep,
    And all goes well for about a week
    But then your coffin begins to leak.
    The worms crawl in and the worms crawl out,
    In through your stomach and out through your snout,
    Your stomach turns a slimy green
    And stuff comes out like whipping cream,
    You mop it up with a piece of bread
    And that's what you eat when you are dead.

33. Within these graves below, three brothers lie
    Whom death quick summoned to eternity;
    In quest of fur they left the shore,
    They little thought they should ne'er see it more.
    Through woods and dreary wastes they made their way
    And with their dogs and guns pursued their prey;
    Fortune their labours crowned with furry spoils,
    Repaid their anxious cares and honest toils.
    But Ah! Before they'd reached their pleasing home,
    Heaven's decree had fixed their wretched doom.
    Exposed to snow and piercing cold oppressed,
    In death's cold arms their souls soon sank to rest.

34. Here lies the body of Mary Ann Best,
    Safe at last in Abraham's breast,
    Which may be great for Mary Ann
    But it's certainly tough on Abraham.

35. This was never known before—
    On this shore.

• • •

3. From *Seldom* by Dawn Rae Downton.

4. "W.W." was W.W. Wareham, a merchant of Placentia Bay. From Les Harris, *Growing Up with Verse*.

5. From Fred Adams, and also quoted in *The Best of the Barrelman*, edited by William Connors.

6. "As I Am Now," was found on a tombstone in the Anglican cemetery, Trinity. Chalked underneath was said to be, "To follow you I'm not content / Until I know which way you went."

7. Said to be from an old Renews graveyard, recorded in *Legacy of Laughter* by Jack Fitzgerald.

8. Solomon Dawe was from St. George's Bay. Also quoted in *The Best of the Barrelman*, edited by William Connors.

9. "Man's Strong Desire" is said to be on a tombstone in Belleoram, Fortune Bay, quoted in *The Best of the Barrelman*, edited by William Connors.

14. Richard and Mary Prichard's tombstone was in Long Beach. Quoted in *The Best of the Barrelman*, edited by William Connors.

15. Mary Ann Ford was from Blackhead Bay, recorded by Les Harris in *Growing Up with Verse*.

16. "Ye Little Ducks" was claimed to have been written by the occupant of a grave on the Great Northern Peninsula. Quoted in *The Best of the Barrelman*, edited by William Connors.

18. Mr. Danner from Long Island, Bonavista Bay, had four wives. Quoted in *The Best of the Barrelman*, edited by William Connors.

19. Eugene Toope in *Eye Your Roots*.

20. From a literacy book in the North West River library.

21. "One Army of the Living God" is from a newspaper memorial from Coley's Point, Bay Roberts, for Sampson Hemsell of Sandwich Bay, Labrador, who died at the age of 24 in 1914, reported in *Them Days*.

22. "To This Give Heed," a variation on "As I Am Now," was written on a wooden marker for Ambrose Brooks, who died in 1852 at the age of 72, at North West River, Labrador. It was reported in *Them Days* that the wooden marker was replaced with a stone one with the same inscription. It is said to be an old trappers' verse and was read at Max McLean's funeral.

23. "Affliction Sore" was on the grave marker of John Joby Junr., who died 1763, aged 33, in the Anglican cemetery at Fogo.

24. "And now his long life's voyage" is on the tombstone of Charles Willis, Eastern Indian Islands, 1945, from Joseph Hackett's *Got a Story to Tell Ye*.

25. "My anvil and my hammer" is on the grave of a blacksmith named Blandford at Greenspond Island, recorded in Smallwood's *Hand Book, Gazetteer and Almanac*.

27. "Just a little cradle" is the epitaph of Lilly Hodder of Ireland's Eye, who died in 1959, reported in Eugene Toope's *Eye Your Roots*.

28. A variation on "Don't Weep for Me Now" is known as the epitaph of the exhausted housewife.

29. From Bob Wakeham's mother, in the *Telegram*, January 14, 2007.

30. From Kevin Jardine in "Those Dear Dim Days" in the *Book of Newfoundland*, Vol. 5.

31. "Weep Not for Us" is from a sampler created by Louisa Purchase of Notre Dame Bay in the late nineteenth century, in memory of her nine sisters and brothers who died of smallpox.

32. When I was small, most children would change the words "horse" to "hearse" because you were unlikely to ever see a white hearse whereas white horses weren't common but did occasionally make an appearance, especially on Orangeman's Day.

33. The three Pardy brothers, Henry (33), John (28), and Jethro (25), settlers at Step-a-Side, Burin, died of exposure while returning from seal hunting. The story went round that they had been killed by Beothuks, and eventually someone went to examine their graves on Pardy Island, formerly Titus Island, and uncovered this epitaph on their tombstone. The details are recorded in the *History of Burin* by the Burin Senior Citizens Association.

34. From Les Harris.

35. "This Was Never Known Before" was chanted responsively and is the equivalent of a hauling shanty—it was used to keep time by women filling in graves, with one line to a shovelful of dirt.

Bibliography

Adams, Fred. *Potpourri of Old St. John's*. St. John's NL: Creative, 1991.

_____. *St. John's: The Last 100 Years*. St. John's NL: Creative, 1988.

Bennett, Margaret. *The Last Stronghold: Scottish Gaelic Traditions in Newfoundland*. St. John's NL: Breakwater, 1989.

Borlase, Tim, ed. *Songs of Labrador*. Fredericton NB: Goose Lane, 1993.

Briffett, Frances B. *More Stories of Newfoundland*. Toronto ON: J.M. Dent and Sons (Canada) Limited, 1939.

Brookes, Chris. *A Public Nuisance: A History of the Mummers Troupe*. St. John's NL: Institute for Social and Economic Research, 1988.

Butler, Victor. *The Little Nord Easter: Reminiscences of a Placentia Bayman*. Ed. Wilfred W. Wareham. St. John's NL: Breakwater, 1980.

Cartwright, George. "Labrador: A Poetic Epistle." *Captain Cartwright and His Labrador Journal*. Ed. Charles Wendell Townsend, MD. Boston: Dana Estes and Company Publishers, 1911. 363-372.

Clarke, Frances A. *Do What You Can: The Memoirs of Frances A. Clarke*. St. John's NL: FAPC Publishing, 2004.

Connors, William, ed. *The Best of the Barrelman*. St. John's NL: Creative, 1998.

Conroy, Elizabeth McGrath. "Johnny." *Inter Nos* 1.4 (June 1925): 40-56.

Cooze, Sandra. *Roses in December: A Treasury of Children's Verse*. St. John's NL: Tuckamore Books, 1996.

Cranford, Garry and Ed Janes. *From Cod to Crab: Stories and History of Hant's Harbour*. St. John's NL: Flanker, 1995.

Dawe, Tom. *Landwash Days*. St. John's NL: Newfoundland Book Publishers, 1980.

_____. *The Yarns of Ishmael Drake*. St. John's NL: Harry Cuff, 1982.

Devine, P.K.; comp. *Devine's Folk Lore of Newfoundland in Old Words, Phrases and Expressions, Their Origins and Meaning*. St. John's NL: Robinson and Co., 1937.

_____. *In the Good Old Days!: Fishing Customs of the Past*. St. John's NL: Harry Cuff, 1990.

Dewling, Clarence and Sarah. "A Riddle-me Evening." *The Telegram*, February 16, 2006.

Dohaney, M.T. *A Fit Month For Dying*. Fredericton NB: Goose Lane, 2000.

Downton, Dawn Rae. *Seldom*. Toronto: McClelland and Stewart, 2001.

Duley, Margaret. *The Caribou Hut*. Toronto: Ryerson Press, 1949.

England, George. *Vikings of the Ice*. Garden City, NY: Doubleday, Page & Co., 1924.

Ennis, John Lou. *Adapting to a Changing Situation in Placentia Bay, Newfoundland*. Portugal Cove NL: ESP Press, 1999.

Evans, Calvin D. *For Love of a Woman: The Evans Family and a Perspective on Shipbuilding in Newfoundland*. St. John's NL: Harry Cuff, 1992.

Fearon, Mary and Lori Fritz. *Over the Big Fat Waves: A Collection of Newfoundland and Labrador Rhymes, Songs and Language Games*. St. John's NL: n.p., 2003.

Finch, Robert. *The Iambics of Newfoundland: Notes from an Unknown Shore*. New York: Counterpoint, 2007.

Fitzgerald, Jack. *A Day at the Races: The St. John's Regatta Story*. St. John's NL: Creative, 2003.

_____. *Legacy of Laughter: A Treasury of Newfoundland Wit and Humour*. St. John's NL: Creative, 2007.

_____. *Treasure Island Revisited*. St. John's NL: Creative, 2005.

_____. *Untold Stories of Newfoundland and Labrador*. St. John's NL: Creative, 2004.

Foote, Luke. *Life's Difficult Moments: The Calm after the Storm*. Ed. Burton K. Janes. St. John's NL: Luke Foote, 1996.

From Caplin Bay 1920 to Calvert 1995. [Newfoundland]: The Committee, 1995.

Froude, John W., Capt. *On the High Seas: The Diary of Capt. John W. Froude, Twillingate, 1863-1939*. St. John's NL: Jesperson, 1983.

Goudie, Elizabeth. *Woman of Labrador*. Ed. David Zimmerly. Toronto ON: Peter Martin Associates, 1973.

Graham, Harry. *Ruthless Rhymes for Heartless Homes*. New York: R.H. Russell, 1898.

Greene, John Carrick. *Of Fish and Family: Family Trees and Family Histories of Tilting, Set against a Background of Historical Developments in the Newfoundland Fisheries, 1700-1940*. St. John's NL: Triumphant Explorations, 2003.

Greenleaf, Elizabeth Bristol and Grace Yarrow Mansfield. *Ballads and Sea Songs of Newfoundland*. Cambridge: Harvard University Press, 1933.

Guy, Ray. *Ray Guy: The Smallwood Years*. Portugal Cove NL: Boulder, 2008.

Guy, Raymond W. *Memory is a Fickle Jade: A Collection of Historical Essays about Newfoundland and Her People*. St. John's NL: Creative, 1996.

Hackett, Joseph B. *Got a Story to Tell Ye: From Newfoundland, Canada on Latitude 49:00 and Longitude 58:00*. [Corner Brook NL]: J.B. Hackett, 1995.

Hambling, Jack. *The Second Time Around: Growing Up in Bay Roberts*. St. John's NL: Harry Cuff, 1992.

Hanrahan, Maura. *The Alphabet Fleet: The Pride of the Newfoundland Coastal Service*. St. John's NL: Flanker, 2007.

Harris, Leslie. *Growing Up with Verse: A Child's Life in Gallows Harbour*. St. John's NL: Harry Cuff, 2002.

Hayman, Robert. *Quodlibits: Lately Come Over from New Britaniola, Old Newfoundland*. London: Elizabeth Allde for Roger Mitchell, 1628.

Hiscock, Philip. "More Than Mummers: The Folklore of Newfoundland Christmas." *Newfoundland Quarterly* (December 2005): 9-11.

History of Burin. N.p.: Burin Senior Citizens Association, 1977.

Hodgins, Charles. *Marching Together: The Recollections of a Padre*. Maine: Ingrid Hodgsins, 1983.

Holmes, Albert N. *A Boat of My Own*. St. John's NL: Harry Cuff, 1980.

Hunt, Rev. Edmund. *Aspects of the History of Trinity: A Personal History of Trinity in the Early 1900s*. Ed. Percy Janes. St. John's NL: Harry Cuff, 1981.

Hunter, Dr. A.C. "The Old Royal Readers: Another View." *Newfoundland Quarterly* 75th Anniversary Special Edition (1976): 232-233.

Hussey, Greta. *Our Life on Lear's Room, Labrador*. Ed. Susan Shiner. [Port de Grave NL]: Robinson-Blackmore for G. Hussey, 1981.

Jardine, Kevin. "Those Dear Dim Days (Almost) Beyond Recall." *The Book of Newfoundland*, Vol. 5. St. John's NL: Newfoundland Book Publishers, 1975. 94-101.

Jarvis, Dale. *Wonderful Strange: Ghosts, Fairies and Fabulous Beasties*. St. John's NL: Flanker, 2005.

Jensen, Albert C. *The Cod: The Uncommon History of a Common Fish and Its Impact on American Life from Viking Times to the Present*. New York: Thomas Y. Crowell Company, 1972.

Jesperson, Ivan F. *Fat-Back and Molasses: A Collection of Favourite Old Recipes from Newfoundland and Labrador*. St. John's NL: Jesperson, 1974.

Kavanagh, Patrick. *Gaff Topsails*. Dunvegan ON: Cormorant Books, 1996.

Keating, Bern. *The Grand Banks*. Chicago: Rand McNally, [1968].

Kelland, Otto. *Dories and Dorymen*. St. John's NL: Robinson-Blackmore, 1984.

Lamson, Cynthia. *Bloody Decks and a Bumper Crop*. St. John's NL: Institute for Social and Economic Research, 1979.

Lannon, Alice and Michael McCarthy. *Fables, Fairies and Folklore of Newfoundland*. St. John's NL: Jesperson, 1991.

Leach, MacEdward. *Folk Ballads and Songs of the Labrador Coast*. Ottawa: National Museum, 1965.

Lee, Sheila. *Let Me Tell You a Story: A Collection of Memories*. St. Mary's NL: n.p., [2002].

_____. *Stories from Shirley's Haven*. St. John's NL: s.n., 2004.

Lethbridge, E. Chesley G.K. *A Life of Challenge (One Labradorian's Experiences)*. Ed. Patricia Way. N.p.: E. Chesley G.K. Lethbridge, 2005.

Little, Lewis C. *Through My Grandfather's Eyes: A View of Bonavista from Bygone Times*. Bonavista NL: XX Press, 2006.

Looking Back: Stories of Fort Amherst. St. John's NL: Fort Amherst Reunion Committee, 1997.

Maclean, Sybil. Letter to the Editor. *Atlantic Guardian*, 1947.

Manuel, Edith M. *Newfoundland, Our Province*. Exeter, England: A. Wheaton, 1952.

Margaret, Len. *Fish and Brewis, Toutens and Tales: Recipes and Recollections from St. Leonard's, Newfoundland*. St. John's NL: Breakwater, 1980.

Martin, Wendy. *Once upon a Mine: Story of Pre-Confederation Mines on the Island of Newfoundland*. Westmount QC: The Canadian Institute of Mining and Metallurgy, 1983.

Martin, Willis P. *Two Outports: A History of Dildo-New Harbour*. St. John's NL: Flanker, 2006.

McFarlane, Lucy. "The Recitation." *Newfoundland Quarterly* (Fall 1984): 18-21.

McGrath, James M. *Words Were Our Toys*. St. John's NL: Jesperson, 1982.

McGrath, Robin. *Bay Boy, Bay Boy! More Nursery Rhymes for Newfoundland Children*. Portugal Cove NL: Stone Cold Press, 2004.

_____. "Labrador Rhymes, Taunts and Parodies." *Them Days* 31.2 (2007):14-18.

_____. *Nursery Rhymes of Newfoundland and Labrador*. Portugal Cove NL: Boulder, 2004.

_____. *Old Horse, Old Horse! Nursery Rhymes for Newfoundland Children*. Portugal Cove NL: Stone Cold Press, 2003.

_____. "Political Rhymes in Newfoundland: A Brief History." *Newfoundland Quarterly* 97.2 (2004): 2-7.

Merrick, Elliott. *True North*. New York: Scrivner's & Sons, 1935.

Morgan, Bernice. *Random Passage*. St. John's NL: Breakwater, 1991.

Murphy, Michael P. *Pathways through Yesterday: Historic Tales of Old St. John's*. Ed. Gerald S. Moore. St. John's NL: Town Crier, c.1976.

Murray, Hilda Chaulk. *More than Fifty Percent: Woman's Life in a Newfoundland Outport, 1900-1950*. St. John's NL: Breakwater, 1979.

O'Hara, Aiden. "The Great Railway Debate." *Newfoundland Quarterly* (Fall 1978): 6-8.

Old Time Songs and Poetry of Newfoundland. Printed by the publishers of *The Family Fireside* for Gerald S. Doyle, November 1927.

Old Ways … Busy Days: A Collection of Profiles and Stories from Seniors in the Labrador Straits. West St. Modeste NL: Partners in Learning, n.d.

O'Neill, Paul. *The Oldest City: The Story of St. John's, Newfoundland*. Portugal Cove NL: Boulder, 2003.

Opie, Iona and Peter, eds. *The Oxford Dictionary of Nursery Rhymes*. Oxford: The Clarendon Press, 1952.

_____. *The Oxford Nursery Rhyme Book*. Oxford: The Clarendon Press, 1957.

Osborne, Evelyn. "'We Never Had a Bed Like That for a Violin! We Had a Bag!': Exploring Fiddlers and Dance Music in Newfoundland: Red Cliff, Bonavista Bay and Bay de Verde, Conception Bay." M.A. thesis, Carleton University, Ottawa, 2003.

Parsons, Cecil H. *Effie's Angels: A Memoir*. Ed. Joyce Hillier-Pritchett. [Grand Falls-Windsor NL]: Robinson-Blackmore, 2002.

_____. *On My Way*. Ed. Joyce Hillier. [St. John's NL]: C. Parsons, c. 2005.

Parsons, John and Burton K. Janes. *The King of Baffin Land: The Story of William Ralph Parsons, Last Fur Trade Commissioner of the Hudson's Bay Company*. St. John's NL: Creative, 1996.

Peters, Helen, ed. *The Plays of CODCO*. New York: Peter Lang, 1992.

Pollett, Ronald. *The Ocean at My Door: And Other Newfoundland Stories*. St. John's NL: Guardian Ltd., 1956.

_____. *The Outport Millionaire*. St. John's NL: Flanker, 1998.

Poole, George. *A Lifetime Listening to the Waves: Memories of a Labrador Fisherman*. St. John's NL: Harry Cuff, 1987.

Pottle, Herbert L. *Dawn without Light: Politics, Power and the People in the Smallwood Era*. St. John's NL: Breakwater, 1979.

Porter, Helen. *Below the Bridge*. St. John's NL: Breakwater, 1979.

Porter, Helen Fogwill. "Poor Jack-o'-lantern." *Globe and Mail*, October 21, 2006.

Pumphrey, Ron. *Human Beans: A Memoir*. St. John's NL: Flanker, 2007.

Quilliam, Tom, ed. *Look 'Ere Me Son: Wits and Bits of Newfoundland*. Grand Falls NL: Robinson-Blackmore, 1977.

Rieti, Barbara. *Making Witches: Newfoundland Traditions of Spells and Counterspells*. Montreal: McGill-Queen's University Press, 2008.

Rockwood, Art. *Newfoundland and Labrador Trivia: The Sequel*. St. John's NL: Harry Cuff, 1994.

Rose, George. *Cod: The Ecological History of the North Atlantic Fisheries*. St. John's NL: Breakwater, 2007.

Rowe, Melvin. *I Have Touched the Greatest Ship*. St. John's NL: Town Crier Books, 1976.

Rowsell, Leander. *An Energetic Newfoundlander*. St. John's NL: Dicks and Co., 1990.

Rumbolt, Bonnie, program coordinator. *Linking the Generations: A Collection of Oral Histories Exerpts from the Battle Harbour Region*. Battle Harbour NL: Battle Harbour Literacy Council, 1998.

Ryan, Shannon. *The Ice Hunters: A History of Newfoundland Sealing to 1914*. St. John's NL: Breakwater, 1994.

Russell, Kelly. *Close to the Floor: Newfoundland Dance Music: 35 Tunes in Musical Notation*. St. John's NL: Pigeon Inlet Productions, [199-].

_____. *The Fiddle Music of Newfoundland and Labrador*. St. John's NL: Pigeon Inlet Productions, c.2001-2003.

Saunders, Gary L. *Free Wind Home: A Childhood Memoir, 1935-1948*. St. John's NL: Breakwater, 2007.

Saunders, Sheila Maud. "Folklore, the School and the Child." M.A. thesis, Memorial University, 1982.

The Savour of Things Past. St. John's NL: On Going Book Committee, 1980-81.

Scott, Clyde. *A History of Little Bay East, Fortune Bay*. [NL]: Maroh, 1997.

Seary, E.R. *Place Names of the Avalon Peninsula of the Island of Newfoundland*. Toronto: University of Toronto Press, 1971.

Smallwood, J.R., ed. *Hand Book, Gazetteer and Almanac: An Annual Reference Book*. St. John's NL: Long Brothers, 1941.

Smith, Christina. *The Easiest Dance Tunes from Newfoundland and Labrador*. N.p.: n.p., n.d.

Sparkes, R.F. *The Winds Softly Sigh*. St. John's NL: Breakwater, 1981.

Stacey, Jean Edwards. *Memoirs of a Blue Puttee: The Newfoundland Regiment in World War One*. St. John's NL: DRC Publishing, 2002.

Story, G.M., W.J. Kirwin, and J.D.A. Widdowson, eds. *Dictionary of Newfoundland English*. Toronto: University of Toronto Press, 1982.

Strowbridge, Nellie K. *The Newfoundland Tongue*. St. John's NL: Flanker, 2008.

_____. *Far From Home*. St. John's NL: Flanker, 2005.

Swansborough, W. *Newfoundland Months*. St. John's, NL: G.S. Milligan Jr., 1896.

Thomas, Gerald. "Etudes de folklore et d'histoire orale chez les franco-terreneuvienas." *Folklore and Oral History*. Ed. Neil Rosenberg. St. John's NL: Memorial University, 1978. 63-72.

Tizzard, Aubrey. *On Sloping Ground*. Ed. J.D.A. Widdowson. St. John's NL: Breakwater, 1984.

Toope, Eugene. *Eye Your Roots: The Chronicles of Ireland's Eye and Rise's Harbour*. Grand Falls-Windsor NL: E and Eye Enterprises, 1997.

Tucker, Otto G. "Midsummer Memories." *The Telegram*, June 24, 2005.

_____. *That Nothing Be Lost*. St. John's NL: Harry Cuff, 2003.

Weir, Gail. *The Miners of Wabana: The Story of the Iron Ore Miners of Bell Island*. St. John's NL: Breakwater, 1989.

Widdowson, John. *Folk Speech*, Book I. St. John's NL: Breakwater, 1983.

Williams, Gordon P. "Plant a Sweet Forget-me-not: Autographs and Memories." *Newfoundland Quarterly* 98.1 (2005): 46-47.

Young, Ron. "Weatherwise." *Downhome* (July 2007): 6-7.